Contents

EASY TURKEY GRAVY
Servings: 28 | Prep: 10m | Cooks: 7m | Total: 17m

NUTRITION FACTS

Calories: 22 | Carbohydrates: 2.5g | Fat: 1g | Protein: 0.9g | Cholesterol: 2mg

INGREDIENTS

- 5 cups turkey stock with pan drippings
- 1 teaspoon seasoned salt
- 1 (10.75 ounce) can condensed cream of chicken soup
- 1/4 teaspoon garlic powder
- 1 teaspoon poultry seasoning
- 1 cup milk
- 1/2 teaspoon black pepper
- 1/3 cup all-purpose flour

DIRECTIONS

1. Bring the turkey stock to a boil in a large saucepan. Stir in soup, and season with poultry seasoning, pepper, seasoned salt, and garlic powder. Reduce heat to low, and let simmer.
2. Warm the milk in the microwave, and whisk in the flour with a fork until there are no lumps. Return the gravy to a boil, and gradually stir in the milk mixture. Continue to cook, stirring constantly, for 1 minute, or until thickened. Be careful not to let the bottom scorch.

YUMMY HONEY MUSTARD DIPPING SAUCE
Servings: 6 | Prep: 5m | Cooks: 8h | Total: 8h5m

NUTRITION FACTS

Calories: 159 | Carbohydrates: 7.3g | Fat: 14.8g | Protein: 0.4g | Cholesterol: 7mg

INGREDIENTS

- 1/2 cup mayonnaise
- 2 tablespoons honey
- 2 tablespoons prepared yellow mustard
- 1/2 tablespoon lemon juice
- 1 tablespoon Dijon mustard

DIRECTIONS

1. Mix the mayonnaise, yellow mustard, Dijon mustard, honey, and lemon juice together in a bowl. Cover and chill in refrigerator overnight.

TZATZIKI SAUCEO

Servings: 8 | Prep: 20m | Cooks: 0m | Total: 20m

NUTRITION FACTS

Calories: 75 | Carbohydrates: 6.4g | Fat: 4.4g | Protein: 3.4g | Cholesterol: 3mg

INGREDIENTS

- 2 (8 ounce) containers plain yogurt
- salt and pepper to taste
- 2 cucumbers - peeled, seeded and diced
- 1 tablespoon chopped fresh dill
- 2 tablespoons olive oil
- 3 cloves garlic, peeled
- 1/2 lemon, juiced

DIRECTIONS

1. In a food processor or blender, combine yogurt, cucumber, olive oil, lemon juice, salt, pepper, dill and garlic. Process until well-combined. Transfer to a separate dish, cover and refrigerate for at least one hour for best flavor.

DRY RUB FOR RIBS

Servings: 8 | Prep: 10m | Cooks: 0m | Total: 10m

NUTRITION FACTS

Calories: 27 | Carbohydrates: 6.7g | Fat: 0.2g | Protein: 0.4g | Cholesterol: 0mg

INGREDIENTS

- 3 tablespoons brown sugar
- 1 1/2 tablespoons ground black pepper
- 1 1/2 tablespoons paprika
- 1 teaspoon garlic powder
- 1 1/2 tablespoons salt

DIRECTIONS

1. Mix together the brown sugar, paprika, salt, black pepper, and garlic powder. Rub into pork ribs. For best results, allow ribs to marinate overnight. Grill ribs as desired.

KALE, QUINOA, AND AVOCADO SALAD WITH LEMON DIJON VINAIGRETTE

Servings: 4 | Prep: 25m | Cooks: 15m | Total: 40m

NUTRITION FACTS

Calories: 342 | Carbohydrates: 35.4g | Fat: 20.3g | Protein: 8.9g | Cholesterol: 2mg

INGREDIENTS

- 2/3 cup quinoa
- 1 tablespoon crumbled feta cheese
- 1 1/3 cups water
- 1/4 cup olive oil
- 1 bunch kale, torn into bite-sized pieces
- 2 tablespoons lemon juice
- 1/2 avocado - peeled, pitted, and diced
- 1 1/2 tablespoons Dijon mustard
- 1/2 cup chopped cucumber
- 3/4 teaspoon sea salt
- 1/3 cup chopped red bell pepper
- 1/4 teaspoon ground black pepper
- 2 tablespoons chopped red onion

DIRECTIONS

1. Bring the quinoa and 1 1/3 cup water to a boil in a saucepan. Reduce heat to medium-low, cover, and simmer until the quinoa is tender, and the water has been absorbed, about 15 to 20 minutes. Set aside to cool.
2. Place kale in a steamer basket over 1 inch of boiling water in a saucepan. Cover saucepan with a lid and steam kale until hot, about 45 seconds; transfer to a large plate. Top kale with quinoa, avocado, cucumber, bell pepper, red onion, and feta cheese.
3. Whisk olive oil, lemon juice, Dijon mustard, sea salt, and black pepper together in a bowl until the oil emulsifies into the dressing; pour over the salad.

CILANTRO-LIME DRESSING

Servings: 16 | Prep: 30m | Cooks: 0m | Total: 30m

NUTRITION FACTS

Calories: 87 | Carbohydrates: 6.4g | Fat: 7g | Protein: 0.1g | Cholesterol: 0mg

INGREDIENTS

- 1 jalapeno pepper, seeded and coarsely chopped
- 2 teaspoons balsamic vinegar
- 1 clove garlic
- 1/2 teaspoon salt, or to taste
- 3/4 teaspoon minced fresh ginger root
- 1/4 cup packed cilantro leaves
- 1/4 cup lime juice
- 1/2 cup extra-virgin olive oil
- 1/3 cup honey

DIRECTIONS

1. Place the jalapeno pepper, garlic clove, and ginger into a food processor or blender; pulse until the jalapeno and garlic are finely chopped. Pour in the lime juice, honey, balsamic vinegar, and salt, add the cilantro leaves; pulse a few times to blend. Turn the food processor or blender on, and slowly drizzle in the olive oil until incorporated into the dressing. Season to taste with salt before serving.

LISA'S FAVORITE CARNE ASADA MARINADE
Servings: 12 | Prep: 20m | Cooks: 10m | Total: 1d | Additional: 1d

NUTRITION FACTS

Calories: 207 | Carbohydrates: 5.7g | Fat: 14g | Protein: 15g | Cholesterol: 25mg

INGREDIENTS

- 3/4 cup orange juice
- 1 tablespoon ground cumin
- 1/2 cup lemon juice
- 1 tablespoon paprika
- 1/3 cup lime juice
- 1 teaspoon dried oregano
- 4 cloves garlic, minced
- 1 tablespoon black pepper
- 1/2 cup soy sauce
- 1 bunch fresh cilantro, chopped
- 1 teaspoon finely chopped canned chipotle pepper
- 1/2 cup olive oil
- 1 tablespoon chili powder
- 3 pounds flank steak

DIRECTIONS

1. Combine the orange, lemon, and lime juice in a large glass or ceramic bowl along with the garlic, soy sauce, chipotle pepper, chili power, ground cumin, paprika, dried oregano, black pepper, and cilantro. Slowly whisk in the olive oil until marinade is well combined. Remove one cup of the marinade and place in a small bowl, cover with plastic wrap and refrigerate for use after the meat is cooked.
2. Place the flank steak between two sheets of heavy plastic (resealable freezer bags work well) on a solid, level surface. Firmly pound the steak with the smooth side of a meat mallet to a thickness of 1/4 inch. After pounding, poke steak all over with a fork. Add the meat to the marinade in the large bowl, cover, and allow to marinate in the refrigerator for 24 hours.
3. Preheat an outdoor grill for medium-high heat, and lightly oil the grate.
4. Remove the steak from the marinade and grill to desired doneness, about 5 minutes per side for medium rare. Discard used marinade. Remove meat from heat and slice across the grain.
5. Pour the one cup of reserved, unused marinade over the hot meat and serve immediately.

STEAK TIP MARINADE

Servings: 8 | Prep: 15m | Cooks: 10m | Total: 1h25m | Additional: 1h

NUTRITION FACTS

Calories: 289 | Carbohydrates: 17.8g | Fat: 14.9g | Protein: 19.8g | Cholesterol: 49mg

INGREDIENTS

- 1/2 cup Worcestershire sauce
- 1 cup barbeque sauce
- 1 cup Italian-style salad dressing
- 2 pounds beef sirloin tip steaks
- 2 teaspoons garlic pepper seasoning

DIRECTIONS

1. In a medium bowl, mix the Worcestershire sauce, Italian-style salad dressing, garlic pepper seasoning, and barbeque sauce. Place the meat in the marinade, and turn to coat. Cover, and refrigerate for at least 1 hour.
2. Preheat grill for high heat.
3. Brush grill lightly with oil to prevent sticking. Place steaks on the grill, and discard marinade. Grill steaks 10 minutes on each side, or to desired doneness.

SUE'S HOT FUDGE SAUCE

Servings: 16 | Prep: 4m | Cooks: 7m | Total: 11m

NUTRITION FACTS

INGREDIENTS

- 1 cup butter
- 1 (12 fluid ounce) can evaporated milk
- 1/3 cup unsweetened cocoa powder
- 1 teaspoon vanilla extract
- 3 cups white sugar

DIRECTIONS

1. Combine butter, cocoa, sugar and evaporated milk in a saucepan over medium heat. Bring to a boil and boil for 7 minutes. Remove from heat; stir in vanilla. Carefully pour hot mixture into a blender and blend for 2 to 4 minutes. Serve immediately. Store in refrigerator.

SPINACH BASIL PESTO

Servings: 24 | Prep: 20m | Cooks: 0m | Total: 20m

NUTRITION FACTS

Calories: 67 | Carbohydrates: 0.8g | Fat: 6.6g | Protein: 1.5g | Cholesterol: 1mg

INGREDIENTS

- 1 1/2 cups baby spinach leaves
- 3/4 teaspoon kosher salt
- 3/4 cup fresh basil leaves
- 1/2 teaspoon freshly ground black pepper
- 1/2 cup toasted pine nuts
- 1 tablespoon fresh lemon juice
- 1/2 cup grated Parmesan cheese
- 1/2 teaspoon lemon zest
- 4 cloves garlic, peeled and quartered
- 1/2 cup extra-virgin olive oil

DIRECTIONS

1. Blend the spinach, basil, pine nuts, Parmesan cheese, garlic, salt, pepper, lemon juice, lemon zest, and 2 tablespoons olive oil in a food processor until nearly smooth, scraping the sides of the bowl with a spatula as necessary. Drizzle the remaining olive oil into the mixture while processing until smooth.

KOREAN BBQ CHICKEN MARINADE
Servings: 48 | Prep: 10m | Cooks: 15m | Total: 25m

NUTRITION FACTS

Calories: 20 | Carbohydrates: 4.9g | Fat: 0.1g | Protein: 0.3g | Cholesterol: 0mg

INGREDIENTS

- 1 cup white sugar
- 1 teaspoon ground ginger
- 1 cup soy sauce
- 1 tablespoon lemon juice (optional)
- 1 cup water
- 4 teaspoons hot chile paste (optional)
- 1 teaspoon onion powder

DIRECTIONS

1. In a medium saucepan over high heat, whisk together the sugar, soy sauce, water, onion powder, and ground ginger. Bring to a boil. Reduce heat to low, and simmer 5 minutes.
2. Remove the mixture from heat, cool, and whisk in lemon juice and hot chile paste. Place chicken in the mixture. Cover, and marinate in the refrigerator at least 4 hours before preparing chicken as desired.

BAR-B-QUE SAUCE
Servings: 8 | Prep: 10m | Cooks: 10m | Total: 30m

NUTRITION FACTS

Calories: 33 | Carbohydrates: 8.2g | Fat: 0.1g | Protein: 0.4g | Cholesterol: 0mg

INGREDIENTS

- 1/2 cup ketchup
- 1 dash hot pepper sauce
- 2 tablespoons brown sugar
- 1 teaspoon garlic powder
- 2 tablespoons Worcestershire sauce
- 1/4 teaspoon mustard powder
- 1 tablespoon cider vinegar
- 1/4 teaspoon salt

DIRECTIONS

1. In a small saucepan over medium heat, stir together the ketchup, brown sugar, Worcestershire sauce, vinegar, hot pepper sauce, garlic powder, mustard powder, and salt. Bring to a simmer, then remove from heat and allow to cool slightly before brushing on your favorite meat.

MEAT-LOVER'S SLOW COOKER SPAGHETTI SAUCE
Servings: 8 | Prep: 20m | Cooks: 8h20m | Total: 8h40m

NUTRITION FACTS

Calories: 264 | Carbohydrates: 18.8g | Fat: 14.8g | Protein: 15g | Cholesterol: 45mg

INGREDIENTS

- 2 tablespoons olive oil
- 1 (6 ounce) can tomato paste
- 2 small onions, chopped
- 1 (14.5 ounce) can Italian-style diced tomatoes
- 1/4 pound bulk Italian sausage
- 1 (14.5 ounce) can Italian-style stewed tomatoes
- 1 pound ground beef
- 1/4 teaspoon dried thyme leaves
- 1 teaspoon dried Italian herb seasoning
- 1/4 teaspoon dried basil
- 1 teaspoon garlic powder
- 1/2 teaspoon dried oregano
- 1/2 teaspoon dried marjoram
- 2 teaspoons garlic powder
- 1 (29 ounce) can tomato sauce
- 1 tablespoon white sugar

DIRECTIONS

1. Heat olive oil in a skillet over medium heat; cook and stir onions and Italian sausage until the sausage is browned, about 10 minutes. Transfer the sausage and onions to a slow cooker. In the same skillet, cook and stir the ground beef, Italian seasoning, 1 teaspoon of garlic powder, and marjoram, breaking the meat up as it cooks, until the meat is browned, about 10 minutes. Transfer the ground beef into the slow cooker.
2. Stir in the tomato sauce, tomato paste, diced tomatoes, stewed tomatoes, thyme, basil, oregano, and 2 teaspoons of garlic powder. Set the cooker on Low, and cook the sauce for 8 hours. About 15 minutes before serving, stir in the sugar. Serve hot.

ABSOLUTELY THE BEST RICH AND CREAMY BLUE CHEESE DRESSING EVER

Servings: 6 | Prep: 10m | Cooks: 0m | Total: 10m

NUTRITION FACTS

Calories: 94 | Carbohydrates: 1.3g | Fat: 8.6g | Protein: 3.1g | Cholesterol: 14mg

INGREDIENTS

- 2 1/2 ounces blue cheese
- 2 teaspoons white wine vinegar
- 3 tablespoons buttermilk
- 1/4 teaspoon sugar
- 3 tablespoons sour cream
- 1/8 teaspoon garlic powder
- 2 tablespoons mayonnaise
- salt and freshly ground black peppe

DIRECTIONS

1. In a small bowl, mash blue cheese and buttermilk together with a fork until mixture resembles large-curd cottage cheese. Stir in sour cream, mayonnaise, vinegar, sugar, and garlic powder until well blended. Season to taste with salt and pepper.

GRANDPA'S CLASSIC CONEY SAUCE

Servings: 12 | Prep: 10m | Cooks: 2h | Total: 2h10m

NUTRITION FACTS

Calories: 186 | Carbohydrates: 12.8g | Fat: 9.2g | Protein: 13.5g | Cholesterol: 46mg

INGREDIENTS

- 2 pounds ground beef
- 1/4 cup prepared yellow mustard
- 1/2 cup chopped onion
- 1/2 teaspoon celery seed
- 1 1/2 cups ketchup
- 3/4 teaspoon Worcestershire sauce
- 1/4 cup white sugar
- 1/2 teaspoon ground black pepper
- 1/4 cup white vinegar

- 3/4 teaspoon salt

DIRECTIONS

1. Place the ground beef and onion in a large skillet over medium-high heat. Cook, stirring to crumble, until beef is browned. Drain. Transfer the beef and onion to a slow cooker and stir in the ketchup, sugar, vinegar and mustard. Season with celery seed, Worcestershire sauce, pepper and salt. Cover and simmer on Low setting for a few hours before serving.

CHOCOLATE SYRUP
Servings: 16 | Prep: 5m | Cooks: 5m | Total: 10m

NUTRITION FACTS

Calories: 85 | Carbohydrates: 21.7g | Fat: 0.7g | Protein: 1g | Cholesterol: 0mg

INGREDIENTS

- 1 1/2 cups water
- 1 dash salt
- 1 1/2 cups white sugar
- 1 teaspoon vanilla extract
- 1 cup cocoa powder

DIRECTIONS

1. Combine the water, sugar, cocoa powder, and salt together in a saucepan over low heat; whisk constantly until the mixture thickens and begins to simmer. Remove from heat and stir the vanilla into the sauce. Serve warm or cover and refrigerate until serving.

ARRABBIATA SAUCE
Servings: 6 | Prep: 15m | Cooks: 20m | Total: 35m

NUTRITION FACTS

Calories: 77 | Carbohydrates: 11.8g | Fat: 1g | Protein: 1.9g | Cholesterol: 0mg

INGREDIENTS

- 1 teaspoon olive oil
- 2 tablespoons tomato paste
- 1 cup chopped onion
- 1 tablespoon lemon juice
- 4 cloves garlic, minced

- 1/2 teaspoon Italian seasoning
- 3/8 cup red wine
- 1/4 teaspoon ground black pepper
- 1 tablespoon white sugar
- 2 (14.5 ounce) cans peeled and diced tomatoes
- 1 tablespoon chopped fresh basil
- 2 tablespoons chopped fresh parsley
- 1 teaspoon crushed red pepper flakes

DIRECTIONS

1. Heat oil in a large skillet or saucepan over medium heat. Saute onion and garlic in oil for 5 minutes.
2. Stir in wine, sugar, basil, red pepper, tomato paste, lemon juice, Italian seasoning, black pepper and tomatoes; bring to a boil. Reduce heat to medium, and simmer uncovered about 15 minutes.
3. Stir in parsley. Ladle over the hot cooked pasta of your choice.

MAKE-AHEAD TURKEY GRAVY
Servings: 8 | Prep: 20m | Cooks: 3h55m | Total: 4h15m

NUTRITION FACTS

Calories: 115 | Carbohydrates: 10.2g | Fat: 6.6g | Protein: 4.1g | Cholesterol: 23mg

INGREDIENTS

- 1 large onion, chopped
- 4 sprigs fresh thyme
- 2 carrots, chopped
- 2 cloves garlic (optional)
- 2 ribs celery, chopped
- 3 tablespoons butter
- 2 teaspoons vegetable oil
- 1/2 cup all-purpose flour
- 2 large turkey wings
- salt and ground black pepper to taste
- 2 tablespoons cold water
- 1 pinch cayenne pepper
- 10 cups cold water

DIRECTIONS

1. Preheat oven to 400 degrees F (200 degrees C).
2. Combine onion, carrots, celery, and vegetable oil in a large roasting pan and toss to coat. Place turkey wings on top of vegetables

3. Place roasting pan in the preheated oven and cook until the turkey wings are browned and vegetables are caramelized and softened, 45 to 60 minutes.
4. Transfer turkey wings and vegetables to a large stockpot. Place the roasting pan over a stovetop burner on medium heat. Pour 2 tablespoons cold water into the pan and bring to a boil, scraping up any browned bits. Transfer mixture to the stockpot and add 10 cups cold water, thyme, and garlic.
5. Bring turkey wing mixture to a boil. Reduce heat to low and simmer, uncovered, until meat falls off the bone, about 3 hours. Skim off turkey fat throughout the process and set aside 2 tablespoons.
6. Strain turkey stock and reserve 6 cups of stock; discard all the solids.
7. Heat butter and 2 tablespoons reserved turkey fat in a large saucepan over medium heat. Sprinkle in flour and cook, whisking continuously, until it begins to smell like cooked pie crust, 2 to 3 minutes. Slowly pour in turkey stock, whisking continuously. Increase heat to high and simmer until thick and warmed through, about 5 minutes. Season with salt, black pepper, and cayenne pepper to taste.

OUR FAVORITE BALSAMIC VINAIGRETTE
Servings: 8 | Prep: 10m | Cooks: 0m | Total: 10m

NUTRITION FACTS

Calories: 133 | Carbohydrates: 3.2g | Fat: 13.5g | Protein: 0.2g | Cholesterol: 0mg

INGREDIENTS

- 1/2 cup olive oil
- 1 shallot, minced
- 1/4 cup balsamic vinegar
- 1 clove garlic, minced
- 1 teaspoon honey
- salt and ground black pepper to taste
- 1 teaspoon Dijon mustard

DIRECTIONS

1. Combine the olive oil, balsamic vinegar, honey, Dijon mustard, shallot, garlic, salt, and black pepper together in a glass jar with a lid. Replace lid on the jar and shake vigorously until thoroughly combined.

SAUSAGE GRAVY
Servings: 8 | Prep: 5m | Cooks: 25m | Total: 30m

NUTRITION FACTS

Calories: 344 | Carbohydrates: 7.9g | Fat: 29.9g | Protein: 10.1g | Cholesterol: 51mg

INGREDIENTS

- 1 pound ground pork sausage
- 3 cups milk
- 3 tablespoons bacon grease
- 1/2 teaspoon salt
- 1/4 cup all-purpose flour
- 1/4 teaspoon ground black pepper

DIRECTIONS

1. Brown sausage in a large skillet over medium-high heat. Set aside, leaving the drippings in the skillet.
2. Mix bacon grease into the sausage drippings. Reduce heat to medium, combine with flour, and stir constantly until mixture just turns golden brown.
3. Gradually whisk milk into skillet. When the mixture is smooth, thickened, and begins to bubble, return the sausage to skillet. Season with salt and pepper. Reduce heat, and simmer for about 15 minutes.

BUTTERMILK SYRUP
Servings: 16 | Prep: 15m | Cooks: 0m | Total: 15m

NUTRITION FACTS

Calories: 137 | Carbohydrates: 21.3g | Fat: 5.9g | Protein: 0.4g | Cholesterol: 16mg

INGREDIENTS

- 1 1/2 cups white sugar
- 2 tablespoons corn syrup
- 3/4 cup buttermilk
- 1 teaspoon baking soda
- 1/2 cup butter
- 2 teaspoons vanilla extract

DIRECTIONS

1. In a saucepan, stir together the sugar, buttermilk, butter, corn syrup, and baking soda. Bring to a boil, and cook for 7 minutes. Remove from the heat, and stir in the vanilla.

ABSOLUTE BEST PANCAKE SYRUP
Servings: 4 | Prep: 5m | Cooks: 5m | Total: 10m

NUTRITION FACTS

Calories: 178 | Carbohydrates: 23g | Fat: 9.4g | Protein: 0.9g | Cholesterol: 25mg

INGREDIENTS

- 1/2 cup butter
- 1 tablespoon corn syrup
- 1 cup sugar
- 1/4 teaspoon ground cinnamon
- 1 cup buttermilk
- 1/2 teaspoon baking soda
- 1 tablespoon vanilla extract

DIRECTIONS

1. Bring butter, sugar, buttermilk, vanilla extract, corn syrup, and cinnamon to a simmer in a large saucepan over medium-high heat. Once simmering, whisk in baking soda, and cook for 10 seconds before removing from heat. Serve warm.

VEGETARIAN GRAVY

Servings: 10 | Prep: 10m | Cooks: 20m | Total: 30m

NUTRITION FACTS

Calories: 134 | Carbohydrates: 6.9g | Fat: 11.2g | Protein: 1.7g | Cholesterol: 0mg

INGREDIENTS

- 1/2 cup vegetable oil
- 4 tablespoons light soy sauce
- 1/3 cup chopped onion
- 2 cups vegetable broth
- 5 cloves garlic, minced
- 1/2 teaspoon dried sage
- 1/2 cup all-purpose flour
- 1/2 teaspoon salt
- 4 teaspoons nutritional yeast
- 1/4 teaspoon ground black pepper

DIRECTIONS

1. Heat oil in a medium saucepan over medium heat. Saute onion and garlic until soft and translucent, about 5 minutes. Stir in flour, nutritional yeast, and soy sauce to form a smooth paste. Gradually whisk in the broth. Season with sage, salt, and pepper. Bring to a boil. Reduce heat, and simmer, stirring constantly, for 8 to 10 minutes, or until thickened.

TZATZIKI SAUCE

Servings: 12 | Prep: 5m | Cooks: 0m | Total: 5m

NUTRITION FACTS

Calories: 33 | Carbohydrates: 1.7g | Fat: 2.5g | Protein: 1.1g | Cholesterol: 1mg

INGREDIENTS

- 8 ounces plain yogurt
- 1/2 teaspoon ground black pepper
- 2 tablespoons olive oil
- 1 tablespoon chopped fresh dill
- 1 tablespoon lemon juice
- 3 cloves pressed garlic
- 1/2 teaspoon salt

DIRECTIONS

1. In a mixing bowl, combine the yogurt, olive oil, lemon juice, salt, pepper, dill and garlic. Blend thoroughly and serve.

MAKE-AHEAD TURKEY GRAVY

Servings: 32 | Prep: 30m | Cooks: 2h | Total: 2h30m

NUTRITION FACTS

Calories: 59 | Carbohydrates: 3.2g | Fat: 2.8g | Protein: 4.9g | Cholesterol: 15mg

INGREDIENTS

- 6 turkey wings
- 1/2 teaspoon dried thyme
- 2 medium onions, peeled and quartered
- 3/4 cup all-purpose flour
- 1 cup water
- 2 tablespoons butter
- 2 quarts chicken broth, divided
- 1/4 teaspoon ground black pepper
- 3/4 cup chopped carrot

DIRECTIONS

1. Preheat oven to 400 degrees F (200 degrees C). Arrange a single layer of turkey wings in a large roasting pan. Scatter the onions over the top of the wings. Roast in the preheated oven for 1-1/4 hours or until wings are browned.

2. Place browned wings and onions in a 5 quart stockpot. Add water to roasting pan and stir, scraping up any brown bits on the bottom of the pan. Pour the the water from the pan into the stockpot. Stir in 6 cups broth, carrot, and thyme. Bring to a boil. Reduce heat to medium-low and simmer uncovered for 1-1/2 hours.

3. Remove wings from the pot and place on a cutting board. When the wings are cool, pull off the skin and meat. Discard the skin and save the meat for another use. Strain contents of stockpot through a large strainer into a 3 quart saucepan. Press on the vegetables to extract any remaining liquid. Discard the vegetables and skim the fat off the liquid. Bring the contents of the pot to a gentle boil.

4. In a medium bowl, whisk flour into the remaining 2 cups chicken broth until smooth. Gradually whisk the flour mixture into the simmering turkey broth; simmer 3-4 minutes or until the gravy has thickened. Stir in the butter and pepper. Serve immediately or pour into containers and refrigerate or freeze.

ROASTED RED PEPPER CREAM SAUCE
Servings: 8 | Prep: 30m | Cooks: 20m | Total: 50m

NUTRITION FACTS

Calories: 206 | Carbohydrates: 5.9g | Fat: 18.9g | Protein: 3.6g | Cholesterol: 42mg

INGREDIENTS

- 2 large red bell peppers
- 2 cups half-and-half
- 2 tablespoons minced garlic
- 1/4 cup grated Romano cheese
- 1/4 cup fresh basil
- 4 tablespoons butter
- 3 tablespoons extra virgin olive oil
- salt and pepper to taste

DIRECTIONS

1. Preheat broiler. Lightly coat the red peppers with olive oil. Grill peppers under the broiler until the skin is blackened, and the flesh has softened slightly. Place peppers in a paper bag or resealable plastic bag to cool for approximately 45 minutes.

2. Remove the seeds and skin from the peppers (the skin should come off the peppers easily now). Cut peppers into small pieces.

3. In a skillet, cook and stir the garlic, basil, and red peppers in 3 tablespoons olive oil over medium heat. Cook for 10 minutes, so that the flavors mix.

4. Place mixture in blender (careful it is hot), and puree to desired consistency. Return puree to skillet, and reheat to a boil. Stir in the half-and-half and the Romano cheese; cook and stir until the cheese melts. Add the butter, and stir until melted. Season with salt and pepper to taste. Simmer for 5 minutes.

SIMPLE BEEF FLAVORED GRAVY

Servings: 6 | Prep: 5m | Cooks: 10m | Total: 15m

NUTRITION FACTS

Calories: 98 | Carbohydrates: 6.1g | Fat: 7.9g | Protein: 1.1g | Cholesterol: 20mg

INGREDIENTS

- 1 1/2 cups water
- 1 onion, chopped
- 3 teaspoons beef bouillon
- 1/4 cup butter
- 1/4 cup all-purpose flour

DIRECTIONS

1. Combine water, bouillon, flour, onion and butter in a small saucepan. Bring to a boil over medium heat and cook until thickened.

CHEESE SAUCE FOR BROCCOLI AND CAULIFLOWER

Servings: 6 | Prep: 5m | Cooks: 10m | Total: 15m

NUTRITION FACTS

Calories: 177.6 | Carbohydrates: 4.3g | Fat: 0g | Protein: 8.7g | Cholesterol: 43.1mg

INGREDIENTS

- 2 tablespoons butter
- 1 1/2 cups shredded Cheddar cheese
- 2 tablespoons all-purpose flour
- 1 pinch salt and ground black pepper to taste
- 1 cup milk

DIRECTIONS

1. Melt butter in a saucepan over medium heat; whisk flour into butter until smooth. Pour milk into butter mixture and stir with a wooden spoon to combine. Cook and stir until mixture thickens, about 3 minutes. Add Cheddar cheese and stir until cheese is melted, about 3 minutes more. Season with salt and pepper.

CREAMY ITALIAN DRESSING

Servings: 12 | Prep: 10m | Cooks: 0m | Total: 10m

Calories: 139 | Carbohydrates: 2.4g | Fat: 14.6g | Protein: 0.2g | Cholesterol: 7mg

INGREDIENTS

- 1 cup mayonnaise
- 3/4 teaspoon Italian seasoning
- 1/2 small onion
- 1/4 teaspoon garlic powder
- 2 tablespoons red wine vinegar
- 1/4 teaspoon salt
- 1 tablespoon white sugar
- 1/8 teaspoon ground black pepper

DIRECTIONS

1. In a blender or food processor, combine mayonnaise, onion, vinegar, and sugar. Season with Italian seasoning, garlic powder, salt, and pepper. Blend until smooth.

QUICK PICKLED JALAPENO RINGS
Servings: 2 | Prep: 5m | Cooks: 20m | Total: 25m

NUTRITION FACTS

Calories: 99 | Carbohydrates: 23.6g | Fat: 0.5g | Protein: 1.1g | Cholesterol: 0mg

INGREDIENTS

- 3/4 cup water
- 1 clove garlic, crushed
- 3/4 cup distilled white vinegar
- 1/2 teaspoon oregano
- 3 tablespoons white sugar
- 10 large jalapeno peppers, sliced into rings
- 1 tablespoon kosher salt

DIRECTIONS

1. Combine water, vinegar, sugar, kosher salt, garlic, and oregano in a saucepan over high heat. Bring mixture to a boil, stir in jalapeno peppers and remove from heat. Let mixture cool for 10 minutes.
2. Pack peppers into jars using tongs, cover with vinegar mixture, cover, and refrigerate until needed.

WHOLE EGG MAYONNAISE
Servings: 16 | Prep: 10m | Cooks: 0m | Total: 10m

NUTRITION FACTS

Calories: 250 | Carbohydrates: 0.1g | Fat: 27.9g | Protein: 0.8g | Cholesterol: 23mg

INGREDIENTS

- 1/2 teaspoon dry mustard powder
- 2 tablespoons white vinegar
- 1/4 teaspoon salt
- 2 cups vegetable oil
- 2 eggs

DIRECTIONS

1. In the container of a food processor or blender, combine the mustard powder, salt, eggs and vinegar. Set the food processor on medium speed and gradually drizzle in the oil while it runs. Transfer to a container with a lid and store in the refrigerator for up to two weeks.

HOMEMADE REFRIGERATOR PICKLES
Servings: 64 | Prep: 20m | Cooks: 10m | Total: 30m

NUTRITION FACTS

Calories: 27 | Carbohydrates: 6.8g | Fat: 0g | Protein: 0.1g | Cholesterol: 0mg

INGREDIENTS

- 1 cup distilled white vinegar
- 6 cups sliced cucumbers
- 1 tablespoon salt
- 1 cup sliced onions
- 2 cups white sugar
- 1 cup sliced green bell peppers

DIRECTIONS

1. In a medium saucepan over medium heat, bring vinegar, salt and sugar to a boil. Boil until the sugar has dissolved, about 10 minutes.
2. Place the cucumbers, onions and green bell peppers in a large bowl. Pour the vinegar mixture over the vegetables. Transfer to sterile containers and store in the refrigerator.

THAI-STYLE PEANUT SAUCE WITH HONEY

Servings: 8 | Prep: 15m | Cooks: 0m | Total: 15m

NUTRITION FACTS

Calories: 143 | Carbohydrates: 11.8g | Fat: 10.2g | Protein: 3g | Cholesterol: 0mg

INGREDIENTS

- 1/4 cup honey
- 2 tablespoons extra-virgin olive oil
- 1/4 cup smooth peanut butter
- 1 tablespoon sesame oil
- 1 tablespoon crunchy peanut butter (optional)
- 2 teaspoons minced fresh garlic
- 3 tablespoons soy sauce
- 1 tablespoon minced fresh ginger root
- 2 tablespoons rice vinegar
- 1 teaspoon crushed red pepper flakes

DIRECTIONS

1. Stir together the honey, peanut butters, soy sauce, rice vinegar, olive oil, sesame oil, garlic, ginger, and red pepper flakes in a small bowl.

BREAD AND BUTTER PICKLES

Servings: 50 | Prep: 1h | Cooks: 30m | Total: 4h30m

NUTRITION FACTS

Calories: 105 | Carbohydrates: 25.6g | Fat: 0.3g | Protein: 1g | Cholesterol: 0mg

INGREDIENTS

- 25 cucumbers, thinly sliced
- 5 cups white sugar
- 6 onions, thinly sliced
- 2 tablespoons mustard seed
- 2 green bell peppers, diced
- 1 1/2 teaspoons celery seed
- 3 cloves garlic, chopped
- 1/2 teaspoon whole cloves
- 1/2 cup salt
- 1 tablespoon ground turmeric

- 3 cups cider vinegar

DIRECTIONS

1. In a large bowl, mix together cucumbers, onions, green bell peppers, garlic and salt. Allow to stand approximately 3 hours.
2. In a large saucepan, mix the cider vinegar, white sugar, mustard seed, celery seed, whole cloves and turmeric. Bring to a boil.
3. Drain any liquid from the cucumber mixture. Stir the cucumber mixture into the boiling vinegar mixture. Remove from heat shortly before the combined mixtures return to boil.
4. Transfer to sterile containers. Seal and chill in the refrigerator until serving.

FAMOUS JAPANESE RESTAURANT-STYLE SALAD DRESSING

Servings: 14 | Prep: 10m | Cooks: 0m | Total: 10m

NUTRITION FACTS

Calories: 82| Carbohydrates: 3.3g | Fat: 7.7g | Protein: 0.2g | Cholesterol: 0mg

INGREDIENTS

- 1/2 cup minced onion
- 4 teaspoons soy sauce
- 1/2 cup peanut oil
- 2 teaspoons white sugar
- 1/3 cup rice wine vinegar
- 2 teaspoons lemon juice
- 2 tablespoons water
- 1/2 teaspoon minced garlic
- 2 tablespoons minced fresh ginger root
- 1/2 teaspoon salt
- 2 tablespoons minced celery
- 1/4 teaspoon ground black pepper
- 2 tablespoons ketchup

DIRECTIONS

1. In a blender, combine the minced onion, peanut oil, rice vinegar, water, ginger, celery, ketchup, soy sauce, sugar, lemon juice, garlic, salt and pepper . Blend on high speed for about 30 seconds or until all of the ingredients are well-pureed.

EASY PESTO
Servings: 6 | Prep: 2m | Cooks: 10m | Total: 12m

NUTRITION FACTS

Calories: 199 | Carbohydrates: 2g | Fat: 21.1g | Protein: 1.7g | Cholesterol: 0mg

INGREDIENTS

- 1/4 cup almonds
- 1/2 cup olive oil
- 3 cloves garlic
- 1 pinch ground nutmeg
- 1 1/2 cups fresh basil leaves
- salt and pepper to taste

DIRECTIONS

1. Preheat oven to 450 degrees F (230 degrees C). Place almonds on a cookie sheet, and bake for 10 minutes, or until lightly toasted.
2. In a food processor, combine toasted almonds, garlic, basil, olive oil, nutmeg, salt and pepper. Process until a coarse paste is formed.

CINNAMON HONEY BUTTER
Servings: 16 | Prep: 5m | Cooks: 0m | Total: 5m

NUTRITION FACTS

Calories: 99 | Carbohydrates: 12.8g | Fat: 5.8g | Protein: 0.1g | Cholesterol: 15mg

INGREDIENTS

- 1/2 cup butter, softened
- 1/2 cup honey
- 1/2 cup confectioners' sugar
- 1 teaspoon ground cinnamon

DIRECTIONS

1. In a medium bowl, combine butter, confectioners' sugar honey and cinnamon. Beat until light and fluffy.

QUICK AND EASY HOLLANDAISE SAUCE IN THE MICROWAVE

Servings: 2 | Prep: 5m | Cooks: 0m | Total: 5m

NUTRITION FACTS

Calories: 257 | Carbohydrates: 1g | Fat: 27.4g | Protein: 2.9g | Cholesterol: 266mg

INGREDIENTS

- 2 egg yolks
- 1 pinch cayenne pepper
- 1/4 lemon, juiced, or to taste
- 1/4 cup salted butter, melted
- 1 pinch salt

DIRECTIONS

1. Beat egg yolks, lemon juice, salt, and cayenne pepper together in a microwave-safe bowl until smooth. Slowly stream melted butter into the egg yolk mixture while whisking to incorporate.
2. Heat in microwave for 15 to 20 seconds; whisk.

BALSAMIC VINAIGRETTE

Servings: 6 | Prep: 10m | Cooks: 0m | Total: 10m

NUTRITION FACTS

Calories: 184 | Carbohydrates: 3.4g | Fat: 18.9g | Protein: 0.3g | Cholesterol: 0mg

INGREDIENTS

- 1/2 cup extra virgin olive oil
- 1 teaspoon ground mustard
- 1/2 cup white balsamic vinegar
- 1 pinch salt
- 1 clove crushed garlic
- ground black pepper to taste

DIRECTIONS

1. In a small bowl, whisk together olive oil, white balsamic vinegar, garlic, and mustard powder. Season to taste with salt and black pepper. Stir in minced fresh herbs if desired.

GREEN SALAD WITH CRANBERRY VINAIGRETTE
Servings: 8 | Prep: 15m | Cooks: 5m | Total: 20m

NUTRITION FACTS

Calories: 218 | Carbohydrates: 6.2g | Fat: 19.2g | Protein: 6.5g | Cholesterol: 11mg

INGREDIENTS

- 1 cup sliced almonds
- 1/2 teaspoon salt
- 3 tablespoons red wine vinegar
- 1/2 teaspoon ground black pepper
- 1/3 cup olive oil
- 2 tablespoons water
- 1/4 cup fresh cranberries
- 1/2 red onion, thinly sliced
- 1 tablespoon Dijon mustard
- 4 ounces crumbled blue cheese
- 1/2 teaspoon minced garlic
- 1 pound mixed salad greens

DIRECTIONS

1. Preheat oven to 375 degrees F (190 degrees C). Arrange almonds in a single layer on a baking sheet. Toast in oven for 5 minutes, or until nuts begin to brown.
2. In a blender or food processor, combine the vinegar, oil, cranberries, mustard, garlic, salt, pepper, and water. Process until smooth.
3. In a large bowl, toss the almonds, onion, blue cheese, and greens with the vinegar mixture until evenly coated.

HOLIDAY CRANBERRY SAUCE
Servings: 16 | Prep: 5m | Cooks: 15m | Total: 8h20m

NUTRITION FACTS

Calories: 111 | Carbohydrates: 28.7g | Fat: 0.1g | Protein: 0.1g | Cholesterol: 0mg

INGREDIENTS

- 4 cups fresh cranberries
- 5 whole allspice berries
- 1 1/2 cups water
- 3 cinnamon sticks

- 5 whole cloves
- 2 cups white sugar

DIRECTIONS

1. Place fresh cranberries and water in a medium saucepan over medium heat.
2. Wrap cloves, allspice berries and cinnamon sticks in a spice bag. Place in the water with cranberries.
3. Cook until cranberries begin to burst, about 10 minutes.
4. Stir in sugar and reduce heat to low. Continue cooking 5 minutes, or until sugar has dissolved. Remove from heat and allow to cool. Discard spice bag. Chill in the refrigerator 8 hours, or overnight, before serving.

MUSHROOM GRAVY

Servings: 6 | Prep: 10m | Cooks: 50m | Total: 1h

NUTRITION FACTS

Calories: 133 | Carbohydrates: 8.9g | Fat: 8.7g | Protein: 5.7g | Cholesterol: 20mg

INGREDIENTS

- 1/4 cup butter
- 1 quart beef stock
- 1 (16 ounce) package sliced mushrooms
- 1 pinch ground black pepper to taste
- salt to taste
- fresh thyme leaves, to taste (optional)
- 1/4 cup all-purpose flour, or as needed

DIRECTIONS

1. Heat butter over medium heat in a saucepan until it foams. Stir in mushrooms. Season with salt. Simmer until liquid evaporates, about 20 minutes.
2. Stir in the flour, cooking and stirring for about 5 minutes. Add about 1 cup of beef stock, stirring briskly until incorporated, then pour in the remaining stock and mix thoroughly. Season with black pepper and thyme. Reduce heat to medium-low, and simmer until thickened, about 30 minutes, stirring often.

HORSERADISH SAUCE

Servings: 8 | Prep: 5m | Cooks: 0m | Total: 5m

NUTRITION FACTS

Calories: 20 | Carbohydrates: 3.2g | Fat: 0.2g | Protein: 0.7g | Cholesterol: 3mg

INGREDIENTS

- 2 tablespoons prepared horseradish
- 3 tablespoons reduced-fat mayonnaise
- 1 tablespoon cider vinegar
- 1/8 teaspoon ground red pepper
- 1 teaspoon dry mustard
- 1/2 cup nonfat sour cream

DIRECTIONS

1. In a small bowl whisk together horseradish, vinegar, mustard, mayonnaise, ground red pepper and sour cream.

FRESH TOMATO MARINARA SAUCE
Servings: 6 | Prep: 15m | Cooks: 1h10m | Total: 1h25m

NUTRITION FACTS

Calories: 147 | Carbohydrates: 16.5g | Fat: 7.4g | Protein: 2.7g | Cholesterol: 0mg

INGREDIENTS

- 3 tablespoons olive oil
- 1 teaspoon oregano
- 1/2 onion, chopped
- 1 teaspoon dried marjoram
- 8 large tomatoes, peeled and cut into big chunks
- 1 teaspoon salt
- 6 cloves garlic, minced
- 1/2 teaspoon ground black pepper
- 1 bay leaf
- 1/4 teaspoon fennel seed
- 1/2 cup red wine
- 1/4 teaspoon crushed red pepper
- 1 tablespoon honey
- 2 teaspoons balsamic vinegar, or more to taste
- 2 teaspoons dried basil

DIRECTIONS

1. Heat olive oil in a stockpot over medium heat. Cook and stir onion in hot oil until softened, about 5 minutes; add tomatoes, garlic, and bay leaf. Bring the liquid from the tomatoes to a boil, reduce to medium-low, and simmer mixture until tomatoes are softened, about 30 minutes.

2. Stir red wine, honey, basil, oregano, marjoram, salt, black pepper, fennel seed, and crushed red pepper into the tomato mixture; bring again to a simmer and cook until herbs have flavored the sauce, about 30 minutes more.
3. Stir balsamic vinegar into the sauce.

MICROWAVE BREAD AND BUTTER PICKLES
Servings: 24 | Prep: 20m | Cooks: 10m | Total: 30m

NUTRITION FACTS

Calories: 9.2 | Carbohydrates: 9.2g | Fat: 0g | Protein: 0.2g | Cholesterol: 0mg

INGREDIENTS

- 1 large cucumber, sliced
- 1 cup white sugar
- 1 teaspoon salt
- 1/2 cup distilled white vinegar
- 1 onion, thinly sliced
- 1/4 teaspoon celery seed
- 1/2 teaspoon mustard seeds
- 1/4 teaspoon ground turmeric

DIRECTIONS

1. In a medium microwave safe bowl, mix cucumber, salt, onion, mustard seeds, white sugar, distilled white vinegar, celery seed and turmeric.
2. Microwave on high 7 to 8 minutes, stirring twice, until cucumbers are tender and onion is translucent.
3. Transfer to sterile containers. Seal and chill in the refrigerator until serving.

RASPBERRY VINAIGRETTE DRESSING
Servings: 12 | Prep: 5m | Cooks: 0m | Total: 5

NUTRITION FACTS

Calories: 118 | Carbohydrates: 9.6g | Fat: 9.2g | Protein: 0g | Cholesterol: 0mg

INGREDIENTS

- 1/2 cup vegetable oil
- 2 teaspoons Dijon mustard
- 1/2 cup raspberry wine vinegar
- 1/4 teaspoon dried oregano

- 1/2 cup white sugar
- 1/4 teaspoon ground black pepper

DIRECTIONS

1. In a jar with a tight fitting lid, combine the oil, vinegar, sugar, mustard, oregano, and pepper. Shake well.

SIMPLE GARLIC AND BASIL PESTO
Servings: 12 | Prep: 15m | Cooks: 0m | Total: 15m

NUTRITION FACTS

Calories: 234 | Carbohydrates: 1.9g | Fat: 23.9g | Protein: 3.7g | Cholesterol: 4mg

INGREDIENTS

- 3 cups chopped fresh basil
- 2/3 cup grated Parmesan cheese
- 1 cup extra virgin olive oil
- 2 tablespoons minced garlic
- 1/2 cup pine nuts
- 1/2 teaspoon chili powder
- 1/8 cup Brazil nuts

DIRECTIONS

1. Place the basil in a blender. Pour in about 1 tablespoon of the oil, and blend basil into a paste. Gradually add pine nuts, Brazil nuts, Parmesan cheese, garlic, chili powder, and remaining oil. Continue to blend until smooth.

BETTER-THAN-OLIVE GARDEN ALFREDO SAUCE
Servings: 4 | Prep: 10m | Cooks: 20m | Total: 30m

NUTRITION FACTS

Calories: 883 | Carbohydrates: 50.8g | Fat: 67.9g | Protein: 20.5g | Cholesterol: 208mg

INGREDIENTS

- 3 tablespoons sweet butter
- 1/4 teaspoon ground white pepper
- 2 tablespoons olive oil
- 1/2 cup grated Parmesan cheese

- 2 cups heavy whipping cream
- 3/4 cup shredded mozzarella cheese
- 2 cloves garlic, minced
- 1 (12 ounce) package angel hair pasta

DIRECTIONS

1. Melt butter and olive oil in a saucepan over medium-low heat. Add cream, garlic, and white pepper; bring to just under a boil. Reduce heat and simmer, stirring often, until mixture is slightly reduced, about 5 minutes.
2. Stir Parmesan cheese into cream mixture and simmer until sauce is thickened and smooth, 8 to 10 minutes. Add mozzarella cheese to sauce; cook and stir until cheese is melted, about 5 minutes.
3. Bring a large pot of lightly salted water to a boil. Cook angel hair in the boiling water, stirring occasionally until cooked through but firm to the bite, 3 to 5 minutes. Drain and transfer pasta to serving plates. Spoon sauce over pasta.

RASPBERRY SAUCE

Servings: 8 | Prep: 10m | Cooks: 5m | Total: 15m

NUTRITION FACTS

Calories: 53 | Carbohydrates: 13g | Fat: 0.2g | Protein: 0.2g | Cholesterol: 0mg

INGREDIENTS

- 1 pint fresh raspberries
- 2 tablespoons cornstarch
- 1/4 cup white sugar
- 1 cup cold water
- 2 tablespoons orange juice

DIRECTIONS

1. Combine the raspberries, sugar, and orange juice in a saucepan. Whisk the cornstarch into the cold water until smooth. Add the mixture to the saucepan and bring to a boil.
2. Simmer for about 5 minutes, stirring constantly, until the desired consistency is reached. The sauce will thicken further as it cools.
3. Puree the sauce in a blender or with a handheld immersion blender and strain it through a fine sieve. Serve warm or cold. The sauce will keep in the refrigerator for up to two weeks.

DELICIOUS APPLE SAUCE

Servings: 2 | Prep: 15m | Cooks: 30m | Total: 45

NUTRITION FACTS

INGREDIENTS

- 2 apples - peeled, cored and shredded
- 1 teaspoon ground cinnamon
- 1/4 cup water
- 3 tablespoons brown sugar

DIRECTIONS

1. Place shredded apples in a medium saucepan over medium low heat. Sprinkle with cinnamon, then add water and cook until the apple bits become soft and mushy.
2. Stir in brown sugar and mix well; if desired, top with ice cream and serve.

HOMEMADE TOMATO SAUCE
Servings: 6 | Prep: 30m | Cooks: 4h | Total: 4h30m

NUTRITION FACTS

Calories: 149 | Carbohydrates: 15g | Fat: 8.9g | Protein: 2.9g | Cholesterol: 10mg

INGREDIENTS

- 10 ripe tomatoes
- 1/4 cup chopped fresh basil
- 2 tablespoons olive oil
- 1/4 teaspoon Italian seasoning
- 2 tablespoons butter
- 1/4 cup Burgundy wine
- 1 onion, chopped
- 1 bay leaf
- 1 green bell pepper, chopped
- 2 stalks celery
- 2 carrots, chopped
- 2 tablespoons tomato paste
- 4 cloves garlic, minced

DIRECTIONS

1. Bring a pot of water to a boil. Have ready a large bowl of iced water. Plunge whole tomatoes in boiling water until skin starts to peel, 1 minute. Remove with slotted spoon and place in ice bath. Let rest until cool enough to handle, then remove peel and squeeze out seeds. Chop 8 tomatoes and puree in blender or food processor. Chop remaining two tomatoes and set aside.

2. In a large pot or Dutch oven over medium heat, cook onion, bell pepper, carrot and garlic in oil and butter until onion starts to soften, 5 minutes. Pour in pureed tomatoes. Stir in chopped tomato, basil, Italian seasoning and wine. Place bay leaf and whole celery stalks in pot. Bring to a boil, then reduce heat to low, cover and simmer 2 hours. Stir in tomato paste and simmer an additional 2 hours. Discard bay leaf and celery and serve.

RED AND GREEN CHRISTMAS JALAPENO JELLY
Servings: 32 | Prep: 20m | Cooks: 10m | Total: 30m

NUTRITION FACTS

Calories: 112 | Carbohydrates: 28.4g | Fat: 0g | Protein: 0.1g | Cholesterol: 0mg

INGREDIENTS

- 1 cup chopped red bell pepper
- 1 1/2 cups apple cider vinegar
- 1/2 cup chopped jalapeno pepper
- 1 (6 fluid ounce) container liquid pectin
- 5 cups white sugar

DIRECTIONS

1. Remove stems, veins and most of the seeds of the bell and jalapeno peppers. Mince peppers in a food processor.
2. In a 5-quart pot over high heat, combine bell peppers, jalapenos, sugar and vinegar. Bring to a rolling boil; boil for 3 minutes. Remove from heat and cool for 5 minutes.
3. Stirring constantly, add the pectin and let mixture continue to cool for 2 minutes more. Now stir for 1 minute.
4. Pour into hot, sterilized jars and top with sterilized lids. Secure lids with bands and allow jars to cool slowly, creating a vacuum seal.

BBQ DRY RUB
Servings: 30 | Prep: 10m | Cooks: 0m | Total: 10m

NUTRITION FACTS

Calories: 60 | Carbohydrates: 15.3g | Fat: 0.1g | Protein: 0.2g | Cholesterol: 0mg

INGREDIENTS

- 1 1/4 cups white sugar
- 1/4 cup freshly ground black pepper
- 1 1/4 cups brown sugar
- 1/4 cup paprika

- 1/2 cup salt

DIRECTIONS

1. In a medium bowl, mix together white and brown sugars, salt, pepper, and paprika. Rub onto pork 10 minutes prior to grilling. Store any leftover rub in a sealed container.

DAD'S HAMBURGER GRAVY

Servings: 6 | Prep: 5m | Cooks: 25m | Total: 30m

NUTRITION FACTS

Calories: 488 | Carbohydrates: 18.8g | Fat: 27.4g | Protein: 39.2g | Cholesterol: 130mg

INGREDIENTS

- 2 pounds lean ground beef
- 2 tablespoons butter or margarine
- 1/2 onion, finely chopped
- 1 teaspoon ground sage
- 5 cups milk
- salt and pepper to taste
- 2 tablespoons chicken bouillon granules
- 1/2 cup all-purpose flour

DIRECTIONS

1. Crumble the ground beef into a large deep skillet over medium-high heat. Cook and stir until evenly browned. Drain most of the grease, leaving just enough to coat the pan. Add the onions, and cook for a few more minutes.
2. Pour 4 cups of the milk into the pan, and stir to scrape up any bits of food that could burn on the bottom of the pan. Mix in the bouillon, butter, sage, salt and pepper. Bring to a boil, and cook for 5 minutes, stirring frequently.
3. Mix the flour into the last cup of milk until smooth. Slowly pour into the skillet, stirring constantly. Simmer for a few minutes to thicken. If the gravy is too thick, thin with a little bit of milk. If it is too thin, simmer longer, or add more flour. Taste and adjust seasonings before serving.

ENCHILADA SAUCE

Servings: 12 | Prep: 10m | Cooks: 30m | Total: 40m

NUTRITION FACTS

Calories: 43 | Carbohydrates: 6.1g | Fat: 2.2g | Protein: 1g | Cholesterol: 0mg

INGREDIENTS

- 7y1 tablespoon vegetable oil
- 1/4 teaspoon ground cinnamon
- 1 cup diced onion
- 3 tablespoons all-purpose flour
- 3 tablespoons chopped garlic
- 5 tablespoons hot chili powder
- 1 teaspoon dried oregano
- 4 1/2 cups chicken broth
- 1 teaspoon ground cumin
- 1/2 (1 ounce) square semisweet chocolate

DIRECTIONS

1. Heat oil in a large saucepan over medium-high high heat. Saute onion until tender. Stir in garlic, oregano, cumin and cinnamon; saute for a few minutes.
2. Stir in flour and chili powder, stirring until sauce thickens. Slowly whisk in chicken broth; reduce until sauce reaches desired consistency. Stir in chocolate until melted and well blended.

DEVIL'S STEAK SAUCE

Servings: 4 | Prep: 10m | Cooks: 15m | Total: 25m

NUTRITION FACTS

Calories: 62 | Carbohydrates: 15.9g | Fat: 0g | Protein: 0.1g | Cholesterol: 0mg

INGREDIENTS

- 2 tablespoons raspberry jam
- 2 tablespoons malt vinegar
- 2 tablespoons brown sugar
- 5 drops hot pepper sauce
- 2 tablespoons Worcestershire sauce
- salt and freshly ground black pepper to taste
- 2 tablespoons tomato sauce

DIRECTIONS

1. In a saucepan over high heat, blend raspberry jam, brown sugar, Worcestershire sauce, tomato sauce, malt vinegar, hot pepper sauce, salt, and pepper. Bring to a boil over high heat, reduce heat to low, and simmer 10 minutes, or until thickened.

HOT PEPPER JELLY

Servings: 48 | Prep: 30m | Cooks: 15m | Total: 1h45m

NUTRITION FACTS

Calories: 88 | Carbohydrates: 22.5g | Fat: 0g | Protein: 0.1g | Cholesterol: 0mg

INGREDIENTS

- 2 1/2 cups finely chopped red bell peppers
- 1 cup apple cider vinegar
- 1 1/4 cups finely chopped green bell peppers
- 1 (1.75 ounce) package powdered pectin
- 1/4 cup finely chopped jalapeno peppers
- 5 cups white sugar

DIRECTIONS

1. Sterilize 6 (8 ounce) canning jars and lids according to manufacturer's instructions. Heat water in a hot water canner.
2. Place red bell peppers, green bell peppers, and jalapeno peppers in a large saucepan over high heat. Mix in vinegar and fruit pectin. Stirring constantly, bring mixture to a full rolling boil. Quickly stir in sugar. Return to full rolling boil, and boil exactly 1 minute, stirring constantly. Remove from heat, and skim off any foam.
3. Quickly ladle jelly into sterile jars, filling to within 1/4 inch of the tops. Cover with flat lids, and screw on bands tightly.
4. Place jars in rack, and slowly lower jars into canner. The water should cover the jars completely, and should be hot but not boiling. Bring water to a boil, and process for 5 minutes.

REFRIGERATOR DILL PICKLES

Servings: 12 | Prep: 10m | Cooks: 15m | Total: 3d25m

NUTRITION FACTS

Calories: 13 | Carbohydrates: 3.1g | Fat: 0.1g | Protein: 0.4g | Cholesterol: 0mg

INGREDIENTS

- 3 1/2 cups water
- 4 cups cucumber spears
- 1 1/4 cups white vinegar
- 2 cloves garlic, whole
- 1 tablespoon sugar
- 2 heads fresh dill
- 1 tablespoon sea salt

DIRECTIONS

1. Stir water, vinegar, sugar, and sea salt together in a saucepan over high heat. Bring to a boil; remove from heat and cool completely.
2. Combine cucumber spears, garlic cloves, and fresh dill in a large glass or plastic container. Pour cooled vinegar mixture over cucumber mixture. Seal container with lid and refrigerate for at least 3 days.

ORANGED CRANBERRY SAUCE
Servings: 24 | Prep: 10m | Cooks: 1h15m | Total: 1h25m

NUTRITION FACTS

Calories: 93 | Carbohydrates: 23.9g | Fat: 0.1g | Protein: 0.3g | Cholesterol: 0mg

INGREDIENTS

- 2 (12 ounce) packages fresh cranberries
- 2 cups orange juice
- 1 orange, zested
- 2 cups packed brown suga
- 3 cinnamon sticks

DIRECTIONS

1. In a medium saucepan, combine cranberries, orange zest, cinnamon, orange juice, and brown sugar. Add enough water to cover, and bring to a boil over high heat. Immediately reduce heat, and simmer for about 1 hour, or until the sauce has thickened. Taste for sweetness, and adjust with additional sugar if necessary. You can not overcook, so continue cooking until you have a good thick consistency. Let mixture cool, then refrigerate in a covered container.

QUICK ALFREDO SAUCE
Servings: 8 | Prep: 10m | Cooks: 5m | Total: 15m

NUTRITION FACTS

Calories: 160 | Carbohydrates: 6.1g | Fat: 13.7g | Protein: 3.6g | Cholesterol: 41mg

INGREDIENTS

- 1/4 cup butter
- 2 cloves garlic, minced
- 1/4 cup all-purpose flour
- 1 tablespoon dried parsley flakes

- 1/2 teaspoon garlic salt
- 1/3 cup grated Parmesan cheese
- 2 cups half and half

DIRECTIONS

1. Melt the butter in a saucepan over medium heat. Whisk the flour and garlic salt into the melted butter until the mixture is smooth. Slowly beat the half and half into the sauce until completely incorporated. Stir the garlic, parsley, and Parmesan cheese into the sauce, whisking continually. Bring the sauce to a simmer; cook, stirring regularly, until the sauce has thickened, 4 to 5 minutes. Use immediately or refrigerate.

GREEK TZATZIKI
Servings: 40 | Prep: 20m | Cooks: 8h | Total: 8h20m

NUTRITION FACTS

Calories: 22 | Carbohydrates: 1.9g | Fat: 1g | Protein: 1.3g | Cholesterol: 1mg

INGREDIENTS

- 1 (32 ounce) container plain low-fat yogurt
- 2 teaspoons grated lemon zest
- 1/2 English cucumber with peel, grated
- 3 tablespoons chopped fresh dill
- 1 clove garlic, pressed
- 1 tablespoon salt, or to taste
- 2 tablespoons fresh lemon juice
- 1 tablespoon freshly ground black pepper, or to taste
- 2 tablespoons extra-virgin olive oil

DIRECTIONS

1. Stir together yogurt, grated cucumber, garlic, lemon juice, and olive oil in a bowl. Add lemon zest, dill, salt, and pepper; whisk until smooth. Pour into a serving dish, cover tightly, and refrigerate 8 hours before serving.

HONEY BALSAMIC VINAIGRETTE
Servings: 12 | Prep: 15m | Cooks: 0m | Total: 15m

NUTRITION FACTS

Calories: 143 | Carbohydrates: 7.8g | Fat: 12.5g | Protein: 0.2g | Cholesterol: 0mg

INGREDIENTS

- 1/2 cup balsamic vinegar
- 1 tablespoon white sugar
- 1 small onion, chopped
- 2 cloves garlic, minced
- 1 tablespoon soy sauce
- 1/2 teaspoon crushed red pepper flakes
- 3 tablespoons honey
- 2/3 cup extra-virgin olive oil

DIRECTIONS

1. Place the vinegar, onion, soy sauce, honey, sugar, garlic, and red pepper flakes into a blender. Puree on high, gradually adding the olive oil. Continue pureeing 2 minutes, or until thick.

TERIYAKI SAUCE AND MARINADE
Servings: 8 | Prep: 10m | Cooks: 20m | Total: 30m

NUTRITION FACTS

Calories: 105 | Carbohydrates: 18.2g | Fat: 0.7g | Protein: 2.3g | Cholesterol: 0mg

INGREDIENTS

- 2/3 cup mirin (Japanese sweet rice wine)
- 7 cloves garlic, minced
- 1 cup soy sauce
- 1 tablespoon minced fresh ginger
- 4 1/2 teaspoons rice vinegar
- 1 dash red pepper flakes
- 1 teaspoon sesame oil
- black pepper to taste
- 1/3 cup white sugar

DIRECTIONS

1. Bring mirin to a boil in a saucepan over high heat. Reduce heat to medium-low, and simmer for 10 minutes. Pour in soy sauce, rice vinegar, sesame oil, and sugar. Season with garlic, ginger, pepper flakes, and black pepper; simmer an additional 5 minutes. Store in a tightly sealed container in the refrigerator.

CINNAMON SYRUP

Servings: 8 | Prep: 5m | Cooks: 10m | Total: 25m

NUTRITION FACTS

Calories: 110 | Carbohydrates: 27.7g | Fat: 0g | Protein: 0.2g | Cholesterol: 0mg

INGREDIENTS

- 1/2 cup white sugar
- 1/2 teaspoon ground cinnamon
- 1/2 cup packed brown sugar
- 1 teaspoon vanilla extract
- 2 tablespoons all-purpose flour
- 1 cup water

DIRECTIONS

1. Stir together the white sugar, brown sugar, flour, and cinnamon in a small saucepan. Stir in vanilla extract and water. Bring to a rolling boil, stirring often. Continue to boil and stir until mixture thickens to syrup consistency. Remove from heat; cool 10 minutes before serving.

BUTTERY ALFREDO SAUCE

Servings: 8 | Prep: 10m | Cooks: 35m | Total: 45m

NUTRITION FACTS

Calories: 771 | Carbohydrates: 6.2g | Fat: 77.3g | Protein: 15.7g | Cholesterol: 253mg

INGREDIENTS

- 1 cup unsalted butter
- 8 ounces freshly shredded Parmesan cheese
- 1 1/2 tablespoons minced garlic
- 2 ounces shredded fontina cheese
- 1 tablespoon all-purpose flour
- 1/2 teaspoon salt
- 4 cups heavy cream
- 1 teaspoon ground black pepper
- 1/4 cup whole milk

DIRECTIONS

1. Melt the butter in a large pot over medium heat. Stir in the garlic and flour, and cook and stir until the garlic is fragrant but not browned, about 1 minute. Whisk in heavy cream and milk, whisking constantly until the mixture is hot and slightly thickened, about 10 minutes. Gradually stir in the Parmesan cheese and fontina cheese. Season with salt and black pepper. Continue to simmer until the cheese has melted and the sauce is thickened, stirring often, 20 to 30 more minutes.

TERIYAKI MARINADE
Servings: 24 | Prep: 10m | Cooks: 0m | Total: 10m

NUTRITION FACTS

Calories: 51 | Carbohydrates: 8.44g | Fat: 1.7g | Protein: 0.8g | Cholesterol: 0mg

INGREDIENTS

- 1 cup soy sauce
- 3 tablespoons vegetable oil
- 1 cup water
- 1/3 cup dried onion flakes
- 3/4 cup white sugar
- 2 teaspoons garlic powder
- 1/4 cup Worcestershire sauce
- 1 teaspoon grated fresh ginger
- 3 tablespoons distilled white vinegar

DIRECTIONS

1. In a medium bowl, mix the soy sauce, water, sugar, Worcestershire sauce, vinegar, oil, onions, garlic powder, and ginger. Stir together until sugar dissolves. Voila – marinade.

AWESOME STEAK MARINADE
Servings: 2 | Prep: 5m | Cooks: 5m | Total: 10m | Additional: 5m

NUTRITION FACTS

Calories: 406 | Carbohydrates: 80.5g | Fat: 11.6g | Protein: 3.9g | Cholesterol: 0mg

INGREDIENTS

- 1 1/2 cups steak sauce
- 1/2 cup honey
- 1 tablespoon soy sauce
- 1/2 teaspoon garlic powde

- 1/3 cup Italian-style salad dressing

DIRECTIONS

1. Into a blender pour in the steak sauce, soy sauce, Italian-style dressing, honey, and garlic powder. Blend for 10 seconds. Pour over any type of steak, cover, and let sit overnight; turning occasionally to coat all sides.

SPAGHETTI SAUCE
Servings: 4 | Prep: 10m | Cooks: 20m | Total: 30m

NUTRITION FACTS

Calories: 81 | Carbohydrates: 11.1g | Fat: 2.6g | Protein: 2.3g | Cholesterol: 0mg

INGREDIENTS

- 2 teaspoons olive oil
- 1 (28 ounce) can peeled and diced tomatoes
- 1/2 small onion, chopped
- 4 teaspoons dried basil
- 2 green onions, chopped
- 4 teaspoons dried oregano
- 2 teaspoons crushed garlic
- 1 teaspoon white sugar

DIRECTIONS

1. In a large saucepan heat oil over medium heat. Saute onion, green onion and garlic. When onions are clear, stir in tomatoes, basil, oregano and sugar. Bring to a boil, reduce heat to low, and simmer for 20 minutes.

SPICY REFRIGERATOR DILL PICKLES
Servings: 12 | Prep: 15m | Cooks: 0m | Total: 10d2h15m

NUTRITION FACTS

Calories: 70 | Carbohydrates: 16.9g | Fat: 0.3g | Protein: 1.6g | Cholesterol: 0mg

INGREDIENTS

- 12 3 to 4 inch long pickling cucumbers
- 1 1/2 tablespoons coarse salt
- 2 cups water

- 1 tablespoon pickling spice
- 1 3/4 cups white vinegar
- 1 1/2 teaspoons dill seed
- 1 1/2 cups chopped fresh dill weed
- 1/2 teaspoon red pepper flakes, or to taste
- 1/2 cup white sugar
- 4 sprigs fresh dill weed
- 8 cloves garlic, chopped

DIRECTIONS

1. In a large bowl, combine the cucumbers, water, vinegar, chopped dill, sugar, garlic, salt, pickling spice, dill seed, and red pepper flakes. Stir, and let stand at room temperature for 2 hours, until the sugar and salt dissolve.
2. Remove the cucumbers to three 1 1/2 pint wide mouth jars, placing 4 cucumbers into each jar. Ladle in the liquid from the bowl to cover. Place a sprig of fresh dill into each jar, and seal with lids. Refrigerate for 10 days before eating. Use within 1 month.

HUGH'S DRY RUB

Servings: 36 | Prep: 15m | Cooks: 0m | Total: 15m

NUTRITION FACTS

Calories: 16 | Carbohydrates: 3.5g | Fat: 0.4g | Protein: 0.7g | Cholesterol: 0mg

INGREDIENTS

- 1/2 cup paprika
- 3 tablespoons onion powder
- 3 tablespoons cayenne pepper
- 6 tablespoons salt
- 5 tablespoons freshly ground black pepper
- 2 1/2 tablespoons dried oregano
- 6 tablespoons garlic powder
- 2 1/2 tablespoons dried thyme

DIRECTIONS

1. In a medium bowl, combine the paprika, cayenne pepper, ground black pepper, garlic powder, onion powder, salt, oregano, and thyme. Mix well, and store in a cool, dry place in an airtight container.

SAVORY TURKEY GRAVY

Servings: 24 | Prep: 5m | Cooks: 15m | Total: 20m

Calories: 8 | Carbohydrates: 1.2g | Fat: 0.2g | Protein: 0.3g | Cholesterol: <1mg

INGREDIENTS

- 5 cups turkey stock
- 1 teaspoon salt
- 1/4 cup all-purpose flour
- 1/2 teaspoon ground black pepper
- 1 cup water
- 1/4 teaspoon celery salt
- 1 teaspoon poultry seasoning

DIRECTIONS

1. In a medium saucepan, bring the turkey stock to a boil. In a small bowl, dissolve flour in water.
2. Gradually whisk into the turkey stock. Season with poultry seasoning, salt, pepper, and celery salt. Bring to a boil, reduce heat, and simmer for 8 to 10 minutes, or until thickened.

KRYSTAL'S PERFECT MARINADE FOR BBQ OR GRILLED CHICKEN

Servings: 7 | Prep: 10m | Cooks: 0m | Total: 10m

NUTRITION FACTS

Calories: 190 | Carbohydrates: 21.1g | Fat: 11.7g | Protein: 1.4g | Cholesterol: 0mg

INGREDIENTS

- 1/2 cup brown sugar
- 2 tablespoons Worcestershire sauce
- 1/2 cup balsamic vinegar
- 2 tablespoons sesame oil
- 1/2 cup soy sauce
- 4 cloves garlic, chopped
- 1/4 cup olive oil
- 1/2 teaspoon ground black pepper

DIRECTIONS

1. Whisk together the brown sugar, vinegar, soy sauce, olive oil, Worcestershire sauce, sesame oil, garlic, and pepper until the sugar has dissolved.

THE BEST THAI PEANUT SAUCE

Servings: 10 | Prep: 15m | Cooks: 0m | Total: 15m

NUTRITION FACTS

Calories: 160 | Carbohydrates: 5.7g | Fat: 13.7g | Protein: 6.5g | Cholesterol: 0mg

INGREDIENTS

- 1 1/2 cups creamy peanut butter
- 1 tablespoon fish sauce
- 1/2 cup coconut milk
- 1 tablespoon hot sauce
- 3 tablespoons water
- 1 tablespoon minced fresh ginger root
- 3 tablespoons fresh lime juice
- 3 cloves garlic, minced
- 3 tablespoons soy sauce
- 1/4 cup chopped fresh cilantro

DIRECTIONS

1. In a bowl, mix the peanut butter, coconut milk, water, lime juice, soy sauce, fish sauce, hot sauce, ginger, and garlic. Mix in the cilantro just before serving. Watch Now.

CHOCOLATE GRAVY

Servings: 8 | Prep: 5m | Cooks: 15m | Total: 20m

NUTRITION FACTS

Calories: 225 | Carbohydrates: 26.1g | Fat: 13.1g | Protein: 3.1g | Cholesterol: 35mg

INGREDIENTS

- 1/2 cup butter
- 3/4 cup white sugar
- 4 tablespoons unsweetened cocoa powder
- 2 cups milk
- 1/4 cup all-purpose flour

DIRECTIONS

1. Melt butter in a skillet over medium heat. Add cocoa and flour; stir until a thick paste is formed. Stir in sugar and milk. Cook, stirring constantly, until thick.

SWEET ZUCCHINI RELISH

Servings: 112 | Prep: 50m | Cooks: 1h10m | Total: 12h | Additional: 10h

NUTRITION FACTS

Calories: 47 | Carbohydrates: 11.9g | Fat: 0g | Protein: 0.2g | Cholesterol: 0mg

INGREDIENTS

- 12 cups shredded unpeeled zucchini
- 2 1/2 cups white vinegar
- 4 cups chopped onion
- 1 tablespoon cornstarch
- 5 tablespoons canning salt
- 3/4 teaspoon ground nutmeg
- 1 red bell pepper, chopped
- 3/4 teaspoon ground turmeric
- 1 green bell pepper, chopped
- 1 1/2 teaspoons celery seed
- 6 cups white sugar
- 1/2 teaspoon ground black pepper

DIRECTIONS

1. Place the zucchini and onion in a large, non-metallic bowl, and sprinkle the salt overtop. Use your hands to evenly mix the salt throughout the zucchini. Cover, and refrigerate overnight.
2. The following day, drain the zucchini in a colander, and rinse well with cool water. Squeeze out excess water and set aside. Place the red and green bell pepper, sugar, vinegar, and cornstarch into a large pot. Add the nutmeg, turmeric, celery seed and pepper. Stir to combine, then add the drained zucchini. Bring to a boil over medium-high heat, then reduce the heat to medium-low, and simmer 30 minutes.
3. Meanwhile, sterilize 7 one-pint jars and lids to hold relish. Pack relish into sterilized jars, making sure there are no spaces or air pockets. Fill jars all the way to top. Screw on lids.
4. Place a rack in the bottom of a large stockpot and fill halfway with boiling water. Carefully lower jars into pot using a holder. Leave a 2 inch space between jars. Pour in more boiling water if necessary, until tops of jars are covered by 2 inches of water. Bring water to a full boil, then cover and process for 30 minutes.
5. Remove jars from pot and place on cloth-covered or wood surface, several inches apart, until cool. Once cool, press top of each lid with finger, ensuring that seal is tight (lid does not move up or down at all).

SLOW COOKER BOLOGNESE

Servings: 8 | Prep: 20m | Cooks: 4h30m | Total: 4h50m

NUTRITION FACTS

Calories: 245 | Carbohydrates: 17.9g | Fat: 13g | Protein: 16.3g | Cholesterol: 44mg

INGREDIENTS

- 2 tablespoons olive oil
- 1 (6 ounce) can tomato paste
- 1 cup finely chopped baby carrots
- 1/2 teaspoon salt
- 1 onion, finely chopped
- 1/2 teaspoon ground black pepper
- 2 cloves garlic, minced
- 1 teaspoon dried basil
- 1 pound lean ground beef
- 1 teaspoon dried oregano
- 1 1/2 cups whole milk, divided
- 1/4 teaspoon crushed red pepper flakes
- 1 (28 ounce) can crushed tomatoes
- 1/4 cup grated Parmesan cheese

DIRECTIONS

1. Heat the olive oil in a large skillet over medium heat, and cook and stir the carrots, onion, and garlic until tender, about 10 minutes. Place the ground beef into the skillet and cook and stir, breaking up the meat as it cooks, until browned. Drain off excess fat from the skillet, and pour in 1 cup milk. Bring to a simmer, reduce heat to medium-low, and simmer until the milk is absorbed, about 15 minutes.
2. Place the beef mixture into a slow cooker, and set the cooker to High. Stir in crushed tomatoes, tomato paste, salt, pepper, basil, oregano, and red pepper flakes, and cook for 2 hours. Mix in 1/2 cup milk and Parmesan cheese, stir well, and cook for 2 more hours.

REMOULADE SAUCE A LA NEW ORLEANS
Servings: 6 | Prep: 20m | Cooks: 0m | Total: 20m

NUTRITION FACTS

Calories: 359 | Carbohydrates: 6.7g | Fat: 37.3g | Protein: 1g | Cholesterol: 14mg

INGREDIENTS

- 1 cup mayonnaise
- 2 tablespoons chopped fresh parsley
- 1/4 cup chili sauce

- 2 tablespoons chopped green olives
- 2 tablespoons Creole mustard
- 2 tablespoons minced celery
- 2 tablespoons extra-virgin olive oil
- 1 clove garlic, minced
- 1 tablespoon Louisiana-style hot sauce, or to taste
- 1/2 teaspoon chili powder
- 2 tablespoons fresh lemon juice
- 1 teaspoon salt, or to taste
- 1 teaspoon Worcestershire sauce
- 1/2 teaspoon ground black pepper
- 4 medium scallions, chopped
- 1 teaspoon capers, chopped (optional)

DIRECTIONS

1. Mix together mayonnaise, chili sauce, mustard, olive oil, hot sauce, lemon juice, and Worcestershire sauce. Stir in scallions, parsley, olives, celery, capers, and garlic. Season with chili powder, and salt and pepper. Cover, and refrigerate.

WOW! SWEET AND SOUR SAUCE
Servings: 6 | Prep: 10m | Cooks: 20m | Total: 30m

NUTRITION FACTS

Calories: 274 | Carbohydrates: 70.3g | Fat: 0.3g | Protein: 1.1g | Cholesterol: 0mg

INGREDIENTS

- 2 cups water
- 1 teaspoon red pepper flakes
- 1 1/2 cups white sugar
- 1 tablespoon soy sauce
- 1 cup ketchup
- 1/2 tablespoon steak sauce
- 1 (8 ounce) can pineapple tidbits, undrained
- 1/2 tablespoon cayenne pepper hot sauce
- 2/3 cup distilled white vinegar
- 3 tablespoons cornstarch

DIRECTIONS

1. Stir water, sugar, ketchup, pineapple, vinegar, red pepper flakes, soy sauce, steak sauce, and hot sauce together in a saucepan over medium heat. Remove 1/2 cup of the sauce to a small bowl; whisk cornstarch into the sauce in the bowl. Bring the sauce in the saucepan to a boil, stir the sauce with the cornstarch into the boiling sauce. Cook, stirring occasionally, until thickened, about 15 minutes. Remove from heat and allow to cool slightly before using.

ORANGE, WALNUT, GORGONZOLA AND MIXED GREENS SALAD WITH FRESH CITRUS VINAIGRETTE

Servings: 6 | Prep: 15m | Cooks: 5m | Total: 20m

NUTRITION FACTS

Calories: 368 | Carbohydrates: 22.9g | Fat: 30.1g | Protein: 5.2g | Cholesterol: 7mg

INGREDIENTS

- 3/4 cup walnut halves
- 1/4 cup white sugar
- 10 ounces mixed salad greens with arugula
- 2 tablespoons balsamic vinegar
- 2 large navel oranges, peeled and sectioned
- 2 teaspoons Dijon mustard
- 1/2 cup sliced red onion
- 1/4 teaspoon dried oregano
- 1/4 cup olive oil
- 1/4 teaspoon ground black pepper
- 1/4 cup vegetable oil
- 1/4 cup crumbled Gorgonzola cheese
- 2/3 cup orange juice

DIRECTIONS

1. Place the walnuts in a skillet over medium heat. Cook 5 minutes, stirring constantly, until lightly browned.
2. In a large bowl, toss the toasted walnuts, salad greens, oranges, and red onion.
3. In a large jar with a lid, mix the olive oil, vegetable oil, orange juice, sugar, vinegar, mustard, oregano, and pepper. Seal jar, and shake to mix.
4. Divide the salad greens mixture into individual servings. To serve, sprinkle with Gorgonzola cheese, and drizzle with the dressing mixture.

TROPICAL SALAD WITH PINEAPPLE VINAIGRETTE

Servings: 6 | Prep: 20m | Cooks: 10m | Total: 30m

Calories: 255 | Carbohydrates: 10.9g | Fat: 22.4g | Protein: 5.3g | Cholesterol: 10mg

INGREDIENTS

- 6 slices bacon
- 1 (10 ounce) package chopped romaine lettuce
- 1/4 cup pineapple juice
- 1 cup diced fresh pineapple
- 3 tablespoons red wine vinegar
- 1/2 cup chopped and toasted macadamia nuts
- 1/4 cup olive oil
- 3 green onions, chopped
- freshly ground black pepper to taste
- 1/4 cup flaked coconut, toasted
- salt to taste

DIRECTIONS

1. Place bacon in a large, deep skillet. Cook over medium-high heat until evenly browned, about 10 minutes. Drain, crumble, and set aside.
2. Combine pineapple juice, red wine vinegar, oil, pepper and salt in a lidded jar or cruet. Cover and shake well.
3. Toss lettuce, pineapple, macadamia nuts, green onions and bacon together in a large bowl. Pour dressing over salad and toss to coat. Garnish with toasted coconut.

BEST PEANUT SAUCE
Servings: 4 | Prep: 5m | Cooks: 0m | Total: 5m

NUTRITION FACTS

Calories: 199 | Carbohydrates: 8.2g | Fat: 16.3g | Protein: 8.6g | Cholesterol: 0mg

INGREDIENTS

- 1/2 cup crunchy peanut butter
- 2 drops hot pepper sauce
- 2 tablespoons soy sauce
- 1 clove garlic, minced
- 1 teaspoon white sugar
- 1/2 cup water

DIRECTIONS

1. In a small bowl, stir together peanut butter, soy sauce, sugar, hot pepper sauce and garlic until well mixed. Gradually stir in water until texture is smooth and creamy.

HOT BACON DRESSING
Servings: 8 | Prep: 20m | Cooks: 8m | Total: 28m

NUTRITION FACTS

Calories: 277 | Carbohydrates: 38.6g | Fat: 12.6g | Protein: 3.3g | Cholesterol: 19mg

INGREDIENTS

- 8 slices bacon
- 1/2 teaspoon salt
- 1 1/2 cups white sugar
- 1/4 cup water
- 3 teaspoons cornstarch
- 1/2 cup white vinegar

DIRECTIONS

1. Place bacon in a large, deep skillet. Cook over medium high heat until evenly brown. Drain, crumble and set aside.
2. In a medium bowl, whisk together the sugar, cornstarch and salt, and slowly pour in water and vinegar, whisking constantly.
3. In a medium skillet, add the crumbled bacon and pour the vinegar mixture over it. Cook over medium heat, stirring constantly, until mixture thickens.

HOT ITALIAN GIARDINIERA
Servings: 10 | Prep: 45m | Cooks: 2d2h | Total: 2d2h45m

NUTRITION FACTS

Calories: 233 | Carbohydrates: 5.9g | Fat: 23.5g | Protein: 1.2g | Cholesterol: 0mg

INGREDIENTS

- 2 green bell peppers, diced
- water to cover
- 2 red bell peppers, diced
- 2 cloves garlic, finely chopped
- 8 fresh jalapeno peppers, sliced
- 1 tablespoon dried oregano

- 1 celery stalk, diced
- 1 teaspoon red pepper flakes
- 1 medium carrot, diced
- 1/2 teaspoon black pepper
- 1 small onion, chopped
- 1 (5 ounce) jar pimento-stuffed green olives, chopped
- 1/2 cup fresh cauliflower florets
- 1 cup white vinegar
- 1/2 cup salt
- 1 cup olive oil

DIRECTIONS

1. Place into a bowl the green and red peppers, jalapenos, celery, carrots, onion, and cauliflower. Stir in salt, and fill with enough cold water to cover. Place plastic wrap or aluminum foil over the bowl, and refrigerate overnight.
2. The next day, drain salty water, and rinse vegetables. In a bowl, mix together garlic, oregano, red pepper flakes, black pepper, and olives. Pour in vinegar and olive oil, and mix well. Combine with vegetable mixture, cover, and refrigerate for 2 days before using.

TOMATO SAUCE
Servings: 8 | Prep: 15m | Cooks: 1h45m | Total: 2h

NUTRITION FACTS

Calories: 116 | Carbohydrates: 13g | Fat: 7.1g | Protein: 2.2g | Cholesterol: <1mg

INGREDIENTS

- 1/4 cup olive oil
- 1 teaspoon anchovy paste
- 1 onion, finely diced
- 1 teaspoon white wine vinegar
- 1 rib celery, finely diced
- 1/2 teaspoon dried Italian herbs
- 1 pinch salt
- 1 pinch red pepper flakes
- 4 cloves garlic, minced
- 1 tablespoon tomato paste
- 2 (28 ounce) cans whole peeled San Marzano tomatoes
- 2 tablespoons chopped Italian flat-leaf parsley
- 2 teaspoons white sugar
- water, or as needed

- 1 teaspoon salt

DIRECTIONS

1. Place olive oil, onion, celery, and a pinch of salt into a large heavy saucepan or Dutch oven over medium-low heat. Cook until onions are very soft, about 15 minutes, stirring occasionally. Mix garlic into onion mixture and cook just until fragrant, about 1 more minute.
2. Pour tomatoes and their juice into a large mixing bowl and use your hands to crush the tomatoes until they look pureed.
3. Mix sugar, 1 teaspoon salt, anchovy paste, white wine vinegar, Italian herbs, and red pepper flakes into vegetable mixture. Raise heat to medium and cook just until liquid has evaporated. Stir in tomato paste and bring to a simmer. Pour in San Marzano tomatoes and parsley. Bring sauce to a simmer, turn heat to low, and simmer for 1 1/2 hours, adding a little water as the sauce cooks down. Stir occasionally.

TZATZIKI SAUCE

Servings: 24 | Prep: 6h | Cooks: 0m | Total: 6h

NUTRITION FACTS

Calories: 15 | Carbohydrates: 1.8g | Fat: 0.3g | Protein: 1.2g | Cholesterol: 1mg

INGREDIENTS

- 2 cups plain yogurt
- 1/4 teaspoon ground black pepper
- 2 cloves crushed garlic
- 1/4 cup chopped fresh mint leaves
- 1/2 teaspoon salt
- 1 large cucumber - peeled, seeded and shredded

DIRECTIONS

1. Use a cheese cloth to strain the yogurt over a bowl for 3 to 4 hours, until most of the water has drained.
2. Press excess liquid out of the shredded cucumber. In a medium bowl, stir together the cucumber and strained yogurt. Mix in the garlic, salt, pepper and mint. Chill the mixture for 1 to 2 hours.

CANNOLI DIP

Servings: 10 | Prep: 10m | Cooks: 0m | Total: 10m | Additional: 10m

NUTRITION FACTS

Calories: 295 | Carbohydrates: 31.8g | Fat: 16.6g | Protein: 7.6g | Cholesterol: 39mg

INGREDIENTS

- 2 cups ricotta cheese
- 1 teaspoon vanilla extract
- 1 (8 ounce) package cream cheese
- 1 cup miniature semisweet chocolate chips
- 1 1/2 cups confectioners' sugar

DIRECTIONS

1. Beat ricotta cheese and cream cheese together in a bowl until smooth; add sugar and vanilla. Continue to stir mixture until sugar is completely incorporated. Fold chocolate chips through the cheese mixture.
2. Cover bowl with plastic wrap and refrigerate until chilled, at least 10 minutes.

HOMEMADE CHICKEN FETTUCCINE
Servings: 4 | Prep: 10m | Cooks: 15m | Total: 25m

NUTRITION FACTS

Calories: 790.7 | Carbohydrates: 46.3g | Fat: 0g | Protein: 53.3g | Cholesterol: 244.6mg

INGREDIENTS

- 8 ounces fettuccini pasta
- 1 teaspoon garlic salt
- 2 tablespoons butter
- 1/8 teaspoon ground black pepper
- 3 skinless, boneless chicken breast halves - cut into chunks
- 1 1/2 cups heavy cream
- 8 ounces mushrooms, sliced
- 1/4 cup grated Parmesan cheese

DIRECTIONS

1. Bring a large pot of lightly salted water to a boil. Add fettuccine and cook for 8 to 10 minutes or until al dente; drain.
2. In a large skillet, brown chicken and mushrooms in butter until chicken is cooked through. Season with garlic salt and pepper. Add whipping cream and cook until thick, stirring constantly. Add parmesan cheese when at desired consistency. Serve over noodles.

BALSAMIC CREAM SAUCE
Servings: 4 | Prep: 5m | Cooks: 20m | Total: 25m

NUTRITION FACTS

Calories: 380 | Carbohydrates: 4.2g | Fat: 38.3g | Protein: 6.4g | Cholesterol: 108mg

INGREDIENTS

- 2 tablespoons olive oil
- 2 teaspoons chicken bouillon granules
- 2 tablespoons butter
- 1 cup heavy cream
- 1/4 onion, minced
- 1/2 cup grated Parmesan cheese
- 2 tablespoons balsamic vinegar

DIRECTIONS

1. Heat olive oil and butter in a saucepan over medium-low heat. Stir in the onion, and cook until it has caramelized to a dark, golden brown, about 15 minutes. Stir in the balsamic vinegar, and cook for 1 minute before stirring in the chicken bouillon and cream. Bring to a simmer, then remove from the heat and stir in the Parmesan cheese until melted.

JALAPENO STRAWBERRY JAM
Servings: 64 | Prep: 40m | Cooks: 20m | Total: 9h

NUTRITION FACTS

Calories: 90 | Carbohydrates: 23.1g | Fat: 0.1g | Protein: 0.1g | Cholesterol: 0mg

INGREDIENTS

- 4 cups crushed strawberries
- 1 (2 ounce) package powdered fruit pectin
- 1 cup minced jalapeno peppers
- 7 cups white sugar
- 1/4 cup lemon juice
- 8 half pint canning jars with lids and rings

DIRECTIONS

1. Place the crushed strawberries, minced jalapeno pepper, lemon juice, and pectin into a large saucepan, and bring to a boil over high heat. Once simmering, stir in the sugar until dissolved, return to a boil, and cook for 1 minute.
2. Sterilize the jars and lids in boiling water for at least 5 minutes. Pack the jam into the hot, sterilized jars, filling the jars to within 1/4 inch of the top. Run a knife or a thin spatula around the insides of

the jars after they have been filled to remove any air bubbles. Wipe the rims of the jars with a moist paper towel to remove any food residue. Top with lids, and screw on rings.

3. Place a rack in the bottom of a large stockpot and fill halfway with water. Bring to a boil over high heat, then carefully lower the jars into the pot using a holder. Leave a 2 inch space between the jars. Pour in more boiling water if necessary until the water level is at least 1 inch above the tops of the jars. Bring the water to a full boil, cover the pot, and process for 10 minutes.

4. Remove the jars from the stockpot and place onto a cloth-covered or wood surface, several inches apart. Allow to cool overnight Once cool, press the top of each lid with a finger, ensuring that the seal is tight (lid does not move up or down at all). Store in a cool, dark area.

EASY DEVONSHIRE CREAM
Servings: 16 | Prep: 15m | Cooks: 0m | Total: 15m

NUTRITION FACTS

Calories: 73 | Carbohydrates: 1.3g | Fat: 7.4g | Protein: 0.7g | Cholesterol: 26mg

INGREDIENTS

- 3 ounces cream cheese, softened
- 1 pinch salt
- 1 tablespoon white sugar
- 1 cup heavy cream

DIRECTIONS

1. In a medium bowl, cream together cream cheese, sugar and salt. Beat in cream until stiff peaks form. Chill until serving.

THE BEST RED ENCHILADA SAUCE
Servings: 14 | Prep: 10m | Cooks: 15m | Total: 1h25m

NUTRITION FACTS

Calories: 70 | Carbohydrates: 6.3g | Fat: 4.7g | Protein: 2g | Cholesterol: 0mg

INGREDIENTS

- 6 dried ancho chiles
- 1 1/2 teaspoons salt
- 1 (6 ounce) can tomato paste
- 1 teaspoon dried oregano
- 1/4 cup corn oil
- 1/4 teaspoon ground cumin
- 2 cloves garlic, minced

- 3 cups beef broth

DIRECTIONS

1. Preheat an oven to 400 degrees F (200 degrees C).
2. Arrange the ancho chiles on a baking sheet and toast in the preheated oven 3 to 4 minutes; remove the stems, pulp, and seeds from the toasted peppers. Place peppers in a bowl and pour enough hot water into bowl to cover completely; allow to soak for 1 hour.
3. Combine the ancho chiles, tomato paste, corn oil, garlic, salt, oregano, cumin, and about 1 cup of the beef broth in a blender; blend until smooth. Pour the mixture into a saucepan with the remaining beef broth and place over medium heat; simmer until heated through, about 10 minutes.

CHIMICHURRI SAUCE

Servings: 12 | Prep: 10m | Cooks: 0m | Total: 10m

NUTRITION FACTS

Calories: 133 | Carbohydrates: 1.3g | Fat: 14.2g | Protein: 0.3g | Cholesterol: 0mg

INGREDIENTS

- 1 cup fresh parsley
- 2 teaspoons ground cumin
- 3/4 cup extra virgin olive oil
- 1 teaspoon salt
- 3 tablespoons red wine vinegar
- 1/2 tablespoon minced garlic
- 2 tablespoons dried oregano
- 1/2 tablespoon pepper sauce (such as Frank's Red Hot)

DIRECTIONS

1. Place the parsley, olive oil, red wine vinegar, oregano, cumin, salt, garlic and hot pepper sauce into the container of a blender or food processor. Blend for about 10 seconds on medium speed, or until ingredients are evenly blended.

JOHNNY'S SPICE RUB

Servings: 25 | Prep: 5m | Cooks: 0m | Total: 5m

NUTRITION FACTS

Calories: 12 | Carbohydrates: 2.2g | Fat: 0.4g | Protein: 0.5g | Cholesterol: 0mg

INGREDIENTS

- 1 tablespoon garlic powder
- 1 tablespoon ground cumin
- 2 tablespoons ground black pepper
- 1 tablespoon brown sugar
- 1 tablespoon salt
- 4 tablespoons ground paprika
- 1 tablespoon mustard powder
- 1/2 teaspoon dried oregano
- 1 tablespoon chili powder

DIRECTIONS

1. In a small, nonporous bowl, combine the garlic powder, ground black pepper, salt, mustard powder, chili powder, cumin, brown sugar, paprika and oregano. Mix well and apply to meat.

EASY CHICKEN FAJITA MARINADE

Servings: 10 | Prep: 15m | Cooks: 20m | Total: 4h35m | Additional: 4h

NUTRITION FACTS

Calories: 259 | Carbohydrates: 5.9g | Fat: 0g | Protein: 27g | Cholesterol: 70.3mg

INGREDIENTS

- 1/2 cup vegetable oil
- 2 tablespoons garlic powder
- 2 tablespoons chili powder
- 1/2 teaspoon paprika
- 2 tablespoons lime juice
- 1/2 teaspoon ground black pepper
- 2 tablespoons honey
- 3 pounds skinless, boneless chicken breasts, cut into strips

DIRECTIONS

1. Whisk vegetable oil, chili powder, lime juice, honey, garlic powder, paprika, and black pepper in a bowl to make a marinade. Place chicken strips into a large resealable plastic bag; pour marinade over chicken. Knead bag to coat chicken with marinade. Squeeze out air, seal bag, and refrigerate 4 hours to overnight.
2. Preheat an outdoor grill for medium-high heat and lightly oil the grate.
3. Remove chicken strips from marinade; discard used marinade.
4. Grill chicken on preheated grill until browned, the juices run clear, and an instant-read meat thermometer inserted into the thickest piece reads at least 160 degrees F (70 degrees C), about 10 minutes per side.

GREEN TOMATO RELISH

Servings: 192 | Prep: 1h15m | Cooks: 45m | Total: 2h

NUTRITION FACTS

Calories: 32 | Carbohydrates: 7.6g | Fat: 0.1g | Protein: 0.5g | Cholesterol: 0mg

INGREDIENTS

- 24 large green tomatoes
- 3 tablespoons mustard seed
- 3 red bell peppers, halved and seeded
- 1 tablespoon salt
- 3 green bell peppers, halved and seeded
- 5 cups white sugar
- 12 large onions
- 2 cups cider vinegar
- 3 tablespoons celery seed

DIRECTIONS

1. In a grinder or food processor, coarsely grind tomatoes, red bell peppers, green bell peppers, and onions. (You may need to do this in batches.) Line a large colander with cheesecloth, place in sink or in a large bowl, and pour in tomato mixture to drain for 1 hour.
2. In a large, non-aluminum stockpot, combine tomato mixture, celery seed, mustard seed, salt, sugar, and vinegar. Bring to a boil and simmer over low heat 5 minutes, stirring frequently.
3. Sterilize enough jars and lids to hold relish (12 one-pint jars, or 6 one-quart jars). Pack relish into sterilized jars, making sure there are no spaces or air pockets. Fill jars all the way to top. Screw on lids.
4. Place a rack in the bottom of a large stockpot and fill halfway with boiling water. Carefully lower jars into pot using a holder. Leave a 2 inch space between jars. Pour in more boiling water if necessary, until tops of jars are covered by 2 inches of water. Bring water to a full boil, then cover and process for 30 minutes.
5. Remove jars from pot and place on cloth-covered or wood surface, several inches apart, until cool. Once cool, press top of each lid with finger, ensuring that seal is tight (lid does not move up or down at all). Relish can be stored for up to a year.

PICKLED BEETS

Servings: 60 | Prep: 30m | Cooks: 20m | Total: 50m

NUTRITION FACTS

Calories: 60 | Carbohydrates: 14.1g | Fat: 0.2g | Protein: 1.2g | Cholesterol: 0mg

INGREDIENTS

- 10 pounds fresh small beets, stems removed
- 1 quart white vinegar
- 2 cups white sugar
- 1/4 cup whole cloves
- 1 tablespoon pickling salt

DIRECTIONS

1. Place beets in a large stockpot with water to cover. Bring to a boil, and cook until tender, about 15 minutes depending on the size of the beets. If beets are large, cut them into quarters. Drain, reserving 2 cups of the beet water, cool and peel.
2. Sterilize jars and lids by immersing in boiling water for at least 10 minutes. Fill each jar with beets and add several whole cloves to each jar.
3. In a large saucepan, combine the sugar, beet water, vinegar, and pickling salt. Bring to a rapid boil. Pour the hot brine over the beets in the jars, and seal lids.
4. Place a rack in the bottom of a large stockpot and fill halfway with water. Bring to a boil over high heat, then carefully lower the jars into the pot using a holder. Leave a 2 inch space between the jars. Pour in more boiling water if necessary until the water level is at least 1 inch above the tops of the jars. Bring the water to a full boil, cover the pot, and process for 10 minutes.

SPINACH ALFREDO SAUCE (BETTER THAN OLIVE GARDEN)

Servings: 5 | Prep: 10m | Cooks: 15m | Total: 25m

NUTRITION FACTS

Calories: 599 | Carbohydrates: 4.9g | Fat: 61.4g | Protein: 9.9g | Cholesterol: 203mg

INGREDIENTS

- 1/2 cup butter
- 1 cup grated Parmesan cheese
- 3/4 cup thawed frozen chopped spinach
- 1 teaspoon garlic powder
- 1 pint heavy whipping cream
- 1 pinch salt and ground black pepper to taste (optional)
- 3 tablespoons cream cheese

DIRECTIONS

1. Heat butter in a saucepan over low heat; cook spinach in the melted butter until warmed, about 1 minute. Add cream and cream cheese to spinach mixture; cook and stir until cream cheese is melted, about 5 minutes.
2. Fold Parmesan cheese and garlic powder into spinach mixture; season with salt and pepper. Simmer until sauce is thickened and smooth, about 10 more minutes.

WEDDING GIFT SPAGHETTI SAUCE

Servings: 30 | Prep: 10m | Cooks: 2h30m | Total: 2h40m

NUTRITION FACTS

Calories: 137 | Carbohydrates: 6.5g | Fat: 10.2g | Protein: 5.9g | Cholesterol: 26mg

INGREDIENTS

- 1/2 cup butter
- 2 teaspoons salt (optional)
- 3 tablespoons olive oil
- 2 teaspoons dried rosemary
- 1 large onion, chopped
- 1 1/2 teaspoons dried oregano
- 3 cloves garlic, chopped
- 1/2 teaspoon ground black pepper
- 1 pound ground beef
- 76 fluid ounces water
- 1 pound mild sausage
- 1 (29 ounce) can tomato puree
- 4 teaspoons Italian seasoning
- 3 (6 ounce) cans tomato paste

DIRECTIONS

1. Heat butter and olive oil together with onion and garlic in a large pot over medium heat; cook and stir ground beef and sausage in the onion mixture until browned and crumbly, 10 to 15 minutes. Stir Italian seasoning, salt, rosemary, oregano, and black pepper into ground beef-sausage mixture; simmer for 20 minutes.
2. Pour water, tomato puree, and tomato paste into ground beef-sausage mixture; simmer, stirring occasionally, over low heat until flavors have combined, at least 2 hours.

STEAK SAUCE

Servings: 12 | Prep: 5m | Cooks: 0m | Total: 5m

NUTRITION FACTS

Calories: 29 | Carbohydrates: 7.1g | Fat: 0.2g | Protein: 0.6g | Cholesterol: 0mg

INGREDIENTS

- 1 1/4 cups ketchup
- 4 drops hot pepper sauce (e.g. Tabasco™)

- 2 tablespoons prepared yellow mustard
- 1/2 teaspoon salt
- 2 tablespoons Worcestershire sauce
- 1/2 teaspoon ground black pepper
- 1 1/2 tablespoons apple cider vinegar

DIRECTIONS

1. In a medium bowl, mix together the ketchup, mustard, Worcestershire sauce, vinegar, hot pepper sauce, salt and pepper. Transfer to a jar and refrigerate until needed.

MUSTARD VINAIGRETTE

Servings: 12 | Prep: 5m | Cooks: 0m | Total: 5m

NUTRITION FACTS

Calories: 168 | Carbohydrates: 1.9g | Fat: 18.2g | Protein: 0g | Cholesterol: 0mg

INGREDIENTS

- 1/2 cup white vinegar
- 2 teaspoons salt
- 1 tablespoon honey
- 2 teaspoons minced garlic
- 1 tablespoon prepared Dijon-style mustard
- 1 cup vegetable oil
- 1/2 teaspoon ground black pepper
- 4 drops hot sauce

DIRECTIONS

1. In a small bowl, whisk together the vinegar, honey, mustard, pepper, salt, garlic, oil and hot sauce until thoroughly combined. Chill until serving.

APPLE WALNUT SALAD WITH CRANBERRY VINAIGRETTE

Servings: 12 | Prep: 20m | Cooks: 0m | Total: 20m

NUTRITION FACTS

Calories: 274 | Carbohydrates: 10.6g | Fat: 26g | Protein: 2.1g | Cholesterol: 0mg

INGREDIENTS

- 1/2 cup chopped walnuts
- 1 tablespoon Dijon-style prepared mustard
- 1/4 cup cranberries
- 1 cup vegetable oil
- 1/4 cup balsamic vinegar
- salt and pepper to taste
- 1 cup red onion, chopped
- 10 cups mixed salad greens, rinsed and dried
- 1 tablespoon white sugar
- 2 Red Delicious apples, cored and thinly sliced

DIRECTIONS

1. Preheat the oven to 350 degrees F (175 degrees C). Spread the walnuts out on a baking sheet in a single layer. Bake for 8 to 10 minutes in the preheated oven, or until lightly toasted.
2. In a food processor, combine the cranberries, vinegar, onion, sugar, and mustard. Puree until smooth; gradually add oil, and season with salt and pepper.
3. In a salad bowl, toss together the greens, apples, and enough of the cranberry mixture to coat. Sprinkle with walnuts, and serve.

HOMEMADE CHICKEN GRAVY
Servings: 8 | Prep: 5m | Cooks: 25m | Total: 30m

NUTRITION FACTS

Calories: 169.7 | Carbohydrates: 6.8g | Fat: 0g | Protein: 1.4g | Cholesterol: 44.5mg

INGREDIENTS

- 1/2 cup unsalted butter
- 1/3 cup heavy cream
- 1/2 cup all-purpose flour
- 1 pinch salt and ground white pepper to taste
- 1 quart cold chicken stock
- 1 pinch cayenne pepper

DIRECTIONS

1. Melt butter in a saucepan over medium-low heat. Whisk in flour until fragrant, 10 to 12 minutes.
2. Gradually whisk in cold stock. Reduce heat to low. Bring gravy to a simmer, and cook and stir until thick enough to coat the back of a spoon, 10 to 15 minutes. Stir in heavy cream, and season with salt, white pepper, and cayenne pepper.

BEEF AU JUS
Servings: 4 | Prep: 5m | Cooks: 10m | Total: 15m

NUTRITION FACTS

Calories: 53 | Carbohydrates: 2.3g | Fat: 1.1g | Protein: 8g | Cholesterol: 17mg

INGREDIENTS

- 1/4 cup beef fat drippings from a prime rib or other roast beef (see footnote)
- 1 1/2 tablespoons all-purpose flour
- 2 cups beef broth
- salt and ground black pepper to taste

DIRECTIONS

1. Melt fat in a skillet over medium-high heat. Whisk flour into beef fat; cook, whisking constantly, until the mixture thickens, about 3 minutes.
2. Pour beef broth into fat mixture; increase heat to high and bring mixture to a boil.
3. Boil mixture until it thickens slightly; season with salt and pepper to taste.

SOUTHERN-STYLE CHOCOLATE GRAVY
Servings: 12 | Prep: 10m | Cooks: 10m | Total: 20m

NUTRITION FACTS

Calories: 90 | Carbohydrates: 17g | Fat: 2g | Protein: 1.9g | Cholesterol: 6mg

INGREDIENTS

- 1/4 cup cocoa
- 2 cups milk
- 3 tablespoons all-purpose flour
- 1 tablespoon butter, softened
- 3/4 cup white sugar
- 2 teaspoons vanilla

DIRECTIONS

1. Whisk the cocoa, flour, and sugar together in a bowl until there are no lumps. Pour the milk into the mixture and whisk until well incorporated. Transfer the mixture to a saucepan and cook over medium heat, stirring frequently, until its consistency is similar to gravy, 7 to 10 minutes. Remove from heat and stir the butter and vanilla into the mixture until the butter is melted. Serve immediately.

CREAMY HORSERADISH GARLIC SPREAD

Servings: 8 | Prep: 5m | Cooks: 20m | Total: 25m

NUTRITION FACTS

Calories: 57 | Carbohydrates: 1.2g | Fat: 5.8g | Protein: 0.6g | Cholesterol: 8mg

INGREDIENTS

- 1/2 cup sour cream
- 1/4 teaspoon ground black pepper
- 2 tablespoons mayonnaise
- 1/8 teaspoon white pepper
- 1 tablespoon prepared horseradish
- 1/8 teaspoon dried dill weed
- 1 clove garlic, minced
- 1/8 teaspoon garlic powder
- 1/4 teaspoon salt

DIRECTIONS

1. Mix together the sour cream, mayonnaise, horseradish, garlic, salt, black and white pepper, dill, and garlic powder in a bowl. Chill in the refrigerator for at least 20 minutes before serving.

MRS ESPY'S ENCHILADA SAUCE

Servings: 8 | Prep: 5m | Cooks: 15m | Total: 20m

NUTRITION FACTS

Calories: 52 | Carbohydrates: 4.1g | Fat: 4.1g | Protein: 0.8g | Cholesterol: 0mg

INGREDIENTS

- 2 tablespoons vegetable oil
- 1/4 cup tomato sauce
- 2 tablespoons all-purpose flour
- salt to taste
- 1/4 cup chili powder
- garlic powder to taste
- 2 cups water

DIRECTIONS

1. Heat the oil in a medium saucepan over medium heat. Stir in the flour and cook for 1 minute, then add the chili powder and cook for 1 more minute. Gradually stir in the water, mixing well with a whisk to make sure you get out all the lumps, then stir in the tomato sauce and season with salt and garlic powder to taste.
2. Reduce heat to low and simmer for 10 to 15 minutes. (Note: If sauce thickens too much, just add a little water to thin it out a bit.)

INGRID'S CAESAR SALAD DRESSING
Servings: 8 | Prep: 10m | Cooks: 4h | Total: 4h10m

NUTRITION FACTS

Calories: 193 | Carbohydrates: 1.5g | Fat: g | Protein: 1.2g | Cholesterol: 8mg

INGREDIENTS

- 1/2 cup mayonnaise
- 1/2 teaspoon dry mustard
- 1/4 cup extra virgin olive oil
- 4 dashes Worcestershire sauce
- 3 tablespoons grated Parmesan cheese
- 2 dashes hot pepper sauce (such as Tabasco®)
- 2 tablespoons blue cheese salad dressing
- 1 pinch cayenne pepper
- 1 tablespoon red wine vinegar
- salt and pepper to taste
- 3 cloves garlic, minced
- 1/4 teaspoon anchovy paste (optional)
- 1 teaspoon lemon juice

DIRECTIONS

1. Beat together the mayonnaise, olive oil, Parmesan cheese, blue cheese dressing, vinegar, garlic, lemon juice, dry mustard, Worcestershire sauce, hot pepper sauce, cayenne pepper, salt and pepper, and anchovy paste (if using) in a bowl until well blended.
2. Cover and refrigerate for 4 hours before serving.

BASIL CREAM SAUCE
Servings: 6 | Prep: 10m | Cooks: 15m | Total: 25m

NUTRITION FACTS

Calories: 285 | Carbohydrates: 3.8g | Fat: 28.2g | Protein: 6.3g | Cholesterol: 50mg

INGREDIENTS

- 2 cups fresh basil leaves
- 1/2 cup grated Parmesan cheese
- 4 cloves garlic, minced
- salt and pepper to taste
- 1/4 cup olive oil
- 1 pint light cream
- 2 ounces pine nuts

DIRECTIONS

1. In a food processor, combine basil and garlic. Begin processing, and pour in olive oil in a thin stream. Process for about 40 seconds, or until mixture begins to emulsify. Add pine nuts and Parmesan, then blend for 1 minute.
2. Heat cream in a saucepan over low heat until simmering. Pour 1/2 of the hot cream into the processor with basil pesto, and pulse for 20 seconds to incorporate. Pour mixture back into cream, and simmer for 5 minutes, or until thickened.

PEACH PRESERVES

Servings: 64 | Prep: 20m | Cooks: 1h | Total: 2h

NUTRITION FACTS

Calories: 59 | Carbohydrates: 15.2g | Fat: 0g | Protein: 0g | Cholesterol: 0mg

INGREDIENTS

- 12 fresh peaches, pitted and chopped
- 4 1/2 cups white sugar
- 1 (2 ounce) package dry pectin

DIRECTIONS

1. Crush 1 cup chopped peaches in the bottom of a large saucepan. Add remaining peaches, and set pan over medium-low heat. Bring to a low boil, and cook for about 20 minutes or until peaches become liquid (my family likes a few bits of peach left) .
2. Pour peaches into a bowl, and then measure 6 cups back into the pan. Add sugar, and bring to a boil over medium heat. Gradually stir in dry pectin, and boil for 1 minute.
3. Remove from heat after 1 minute, and transfer to sterilized jars. Process in hot water bath canner for 10 minutes. Let cool, and place on shelf.

CREAMY WHITE WINE SAUCE

Servings: 8 | Prep: 15m | Cooks: 0m | Total: 15m

NUTRITION FACTS

Calories: 129 | Carbohydrates: 3g | Fat: 11g | Protein: 0.8g | Cholesterol: 41mg

INGREDIENTS

- 1 cup heavy whipping cream
- 1 teaspoon salt
- 3/4 cup white wine
- 1 teaspoon dried parsley
- 2 tablespoons all-purpose flour

DIRECTIONS

1. In a medium saucepan over medium high heat, combine the cream, wine, flour, salt and parsley. Stir all together bring to a boil.
2. Reduce heat to low and simmer until thickened.

CHICKEN FAJITA MARINADE
Servings: 6 | Prep: 15m | Cooks: 0m | Total: 15m

NUTRITION FACTS

Calories: 41 | Carbohydrates: 4.7g | Fat: 2.3g | Protein: 0.2g | Cholesterol: 0mg

INGREDIENTS

- 1/4 cup beer
- 1 tablespoon Worcestershire sauce
- 1/3 cup fresh lime juice
- 1 tablespoon chopped cilantro
- 1 tablespoon olive oil
- 1/2 teaspoon ground cumin
- 2 cloves garlic, minced
- salt to taste
- 1 tablespoon brown sugar

DIRECTIONS

1. To prepare the marinade, stir together beer, lime juice, olive oil, garlic, brown sugar, Worcestershire sauce, cilantro, cumin, and salt; mix well.
2. To use marinade, pour into a resealable plastic bag, add up to 1 1/2 pounds of chicken breast, and mix until chicken is well coated. Marinate for 1 to 3 hours in the refrigerator.

DRY RANCH STYLE SEASONING FOR DIP OR DRESSING

Servings: 6 | Prep: 5m | Cooks: 4h | Total: 4h5m

NUTRITION FACTS

Calories: 3 | Carbohydrates: 0.6g | Fat: 0g | Protein: 0.1g | Cholesterol: 0mg

INGREDIENTS

- 1 teaspoon dried parsley
- 1/2 teaspoon garlic powder
- 3/4 teaspoon ground black pepper
- 1/4 teaspoon onion powder
- 1 teaspoon seasoned salt
- 1/8 teaspoon dried thyme

DIRECTIONS

1. In a small bowl, stir together the parsley, pepper, seasoned salt, garlic powder, onion powder and thyme. Use as a substitute for Ranch Dressing Mix.

MARINARA SAUCE

Servings: 4 | Prep: 10m | Cooks: 25m | Total: 35m

NUTRITION FACTS

Calories: 159 | Carbohydrates: 10.7g | Fat: 10.5g | Protein: 2g | Cholesterol: 0mg

INGREDIENTS

- 3 tablespoons extra virgin olive oil
- 1/2 cup water
- 3 cloves garlic, sliced
- 1 teaspoon salt
- 1 (16 ounce) can crushed tomatoes
- 1 teaspoon white sugar
- 1/2 cup red wine
- 6 leaves fresh basil leaves, torn

DIRECTIONS

1. Heat oil in a large non-stick skillet over low heat and saute garlic for about 2 minutes; be careful not to burn. Just as the garlic begins to turn brown, remove pan from heat. Allow pan to cool, and add

tomatoes, wine, water, salt and sugar. Cook over medium-high heat and bring to a boil. Reduce heat to low and simmer, covered, about 20 minutes. Remove from heat and stir in basil.

THE BEST LEMON VINAIGRETTE
Servings: 8 | Prep: 10m | Cooks: 0m | Total: 10m

NUTRITION FACTS

Calories: 128 | Carbohydrates: 1.9g | Fat: 13.5g | Protein: 0.1g | Cholesterol: 0mg

INGREDIENTS

- 1/4 cup red wine vinegar
- 1/2 teaspoon kosher salt
- 2 tablespoons Dijon mustard
- 1/4 teaspoon ground black pepper
- 1 teaspoon dried oregano
- 1/2 cup olive oil
- 1 clove garlic, minced
- 2 tablespoons fresh lemon juice

DIRECTIONS

1. Whisk red wine vinegar, Dijon mustard, oregano, garlic, salt, and black pepper together in a small bowl. Slowly stream olive oil into the vinegar mixture while whisking briskly. Beat lemon juice into the mixture.
2. Pour dressing into a sealable jar or bottle, seal, and shake until emulsified.

SIMPLE TERIYAKI SAUCE
Servings: 12 | Prep: 5m | Cooks: 6m | Total: 11m

NUTRITION FACTS

Calories: 21 | Carbohydrates: 5g | Fat: 0g | Protein: 0.4g | Cholesterol: 0mg

INGREDIENTS

- 1 cup water
- 1/2 teaspoon ground ginger
- 1/4 cup soy sauce
- 1/4 teaspoon garlic powder
- 5 teaspoons packed brown sugar
- 2 tablespoons cornstarch
- 1 tablespoon honey, or more to taste

- 1/4 cup cold water

DIRECTIONS

1. Combine 1 cup water, soy sauce, brown sugar, honey, ginger, and garlic powder in a saucepan over medium heat. Cook until nearly heated through, about 1 minute.
2. Mix cornstarch and 1/4 cold water together in a cup; stir until dissolved. Add to the saucepan. Cook and stir sauce until thickened, 5 to 7 minutes.

SPAGHETTI SAUCE
Servings: 8 | Prep: 10m | Cooks: 1h5m | Total: 1h15m

NUTRITION FACTS

Calories: 169 | Carbohydrates: 13.1g | Fat: 8.2g | Protein: 12.4g | Cholesterol: 34mg

INGREDIENTS

- 1 pound lean ground beef
- 1 tablespoon dried basil
- 1/4 cup chopped onion
- 1 tablespoon garlic powder
- 2 (14.5 ounce) cans stewed tomatoes
- 1 tablespoon dried oregano
- 1 (6 ounce) can tomato paste
- 1 (4.5 ounce) can mushrooms, drained

DIRECTIONS

1. In a large saucepan over medium heat, cook ground beef with onion until brown; drain. Stir tomatoes, tomato paste, basil, garlic powder, oregano and mushrooms into beef mixture. Bring to a boil, then reduce heat to low and simmer one hour. Serve over hot pasta.

FRESH TOMATO BASIL SAUCE
Servings: 6 | Prep: 20m | Cooks: 2h | Total: 2h20m

NUTRITION FACTS

Calories: 330 | Carbohydrates: 37.8g | Fat: 20.6g | Protein: 6.9g | Cholesterol: 0mg

INGREDIENTS

- 8 pounds tomatoes, seeded and diced
- 3 cloves garlic, minced

- 1/4 cup chopped fresh basil
- 1/2 cup olive oil
- 1 large onion, minced
- salt and pepper to taste

DIRECTIONS

1. In large saucepan, cook tomatoes and basil over medium-low heat until tomatoes are soft.
2. Meanwhile, in medium skillet, saute onion and garlic in olive oil until onions are translucent.
3. Add onion mixture to tomato mixture and add salt and pepper. Let simmer on low heat for 2 hours or until thick.

THE BEST MARINADE AROUND
Servings: 1 | Prep: 5m | Cooks: 1h | Total: 1h5m

NUTRITION FACTS

Calories: 571 | Carbohydrates: 22.3g | Fat: 54.4g | Protein: 9.5g | Cholesterol: 0mg

INGREDIENTS

- 1/2 cup soy sauce
- 1/4 cup olive oil
- 1 lemon, juiced
- 1 clove garlic, crushed

DIRECTIONS

1. Mix together soy sauce, olive oil, lemon juice, and garlic. Pour over meat, and refrigerate for 1 hour before preparing as desired.

RHUBARB JAM
Servings: 32 | Prep: 25m | Cooks: 45m | Total: 1h10m

NUTRITION FACTS

Calories: 57 | Carbohydrates: 14.4g | Fat: 0.1g | Protein: 0.3g | Cholesterol: 0mg

INGREDIENTS

- 2 1/2 pounds fresh rhubarb, chopped
- 1/3 cup orange juice
- 2 cups white sugar
- 1/2 cup water

- 2 teaspoons grated orange zest

DIRECTIONS

1. In a saucepan, combine the rhubarb, sugar, orange zest, orange juice and water. Bring to a boil, then cook over medium-low heat for 45 minutes, stirring occasionally, or until thick. It will thicken more as it cools.
2. Ladle into hot sterile jars, and seal with lids and rings. Store opened jars in the refrigerator.

SPRING ROLL DIPPING SAUCE
Servings: 4 | Prep: 5m | Cooks: 5m | Total: 1h10m

NUTRITION FACTS

Calories: 35 | Carbohydrates: 5.6g | Fat: 0.9g | Protein: 1.3g | Cholesterol: <1mg

INGREDIENTS

- 1/4 cup soy sauce
- 1 teaspoon green onions, chopped
- 2 tablespoons hoisin sauce, or more as needed
- 1/2 teaspoon toasted sesame oil
- 1 tablespoon water
- 1/2 teaspoon white sugar
- 1 clove garlic, minced
- 1/4 teaspoon minced fresh ginger

DIRECTIONS

1. Combine soy sauce, hoisin sauce, water, garlic, green onions, sesame oil, sugar, and ginger in a small mixing bowl. Mix well, adding additional hoisin sauce to thicken mixture to your desired consistency if needed. Cover the sauce and refrigerate for 1 to 2 hours to allow flavors to blend.
2. Before serving, pour mixture into a small saucepan and heat. Serve warm.

CHUNKY MARINARA SAUCE
Servings: 6 | Prep: 15m | Cooks: 20m | Total: 35m

NUTRITION FACTS

Calories: 54 | Carbohydrates: 6.9g | Fat: 2.4g | Protein: 1.3g | Cholesterol: 0mg

INGREDIENTS

- 1 tablespoon olive oil
- 1 (8 ounce) can tomato sauce

- 1 onion, chopped
- 1 teaspoon white sugar
- 1 clove garlic, chopped
- 1/2 teaspoon dried oregano
- 1 (14.5 ounce) can peeled and diced tomatoes
- 1/4 teaspoon salt

DIRECTIONS

1. Heat olive oil in a saucepan over medium-high heat. Add onion and garlic and cook 2 to 4 minutes until crisp-tender, stirring frequently.
2. Mix in diced tomatoes, tomato sauce, sugar, oregano and salt. Bring to a boil. Reduce heat to low and simmer 15 to 20 minutes or until flavors are blended, stirring frequently.

CHIMICHURRI SAUCE

Servings: 4 | Prep: 15m | Cooks: 0m | Total: 15m

NUTRITION FACTS

Calories: 255 | Carbohydrates: 3g | Fat: 27.3g | Protein: 1g | Cholesterol: 0mg

INGREDIENTS

- 1/2 cup olive oil
- 1/4 teaspoon red pepper flakes
- 4 cloves garlic, chopped, or more to taste
- 1/4 teaspoon freshly ground black pepper
- 3 tablespoons white wine vinegar, or more to taste
- 1/2 cup fresh cilantro leaves
- 1/2 teaspoon salt, or to taste
- 1/4 cup fresh oregano leaves
- 1/4 teaspoon ground cumin
- 1 bunch flat-leaf Italian parsley, stems removed

DIRECTIONS

1. Combine oil, garlic, vinegar, salt, cumin, red pepper flakes, black pepper, cilantro, oregano, and parsley in a blender.
2. Pulse blender 2 to 3 times; scrape down the sides using a rubber spatula. Repeat pulsing and scraping process until a thick sauce forms, about 12 times.

CREAMY ITALIAN DRESSING

Servings: 8 | Prep: 5m | Cooks: 0m | Total: 5m

NUTRITION FACTS

Calories: 168 | Carbohydrates: 1.8g | Fat: 18.1g | Protein: 0.2g | Cholesterol: 8mg

INGREDIENTS

- 3/4 cup mayonnaise
- 1 teaspoon Worcestershire sauce
- 1 tablespoon red wine vinegar
- 1/2 teaspoon dried oregano
- 1 tablespoon lemon juice
- 1 teaspoon white sugar
- 1 tablespoon vegetable oil
- 1 clove garlic, chopped
- 1 tablespoon water

DIRECTIONS

1. In a small bowl, whisk together the mayonnaise, vinegar, lemon juice, oil, water, Worcestershire sauce, oregano, sugar and garlic until evenly combined. Chill before serving.

MAMA'S BALSAMIC VINAIGRETTE
Servings: 12 | Prep: 10m | Cooks: 0m | Total: 10m

NUTRITION FACTS

Calories: 137 | Carbohydrates: 2.7g | Fat: 14g | Protein: 0.1g | Cholesterol: 0mg

INGREDIENTS

- 3/4 cup extra virgin olive oil
- 2 teaspoons Dijon mustard
- 3/4 cup balsamic vinegar
- 1 pinch salt
- 1 clove garlic, crushed or to taste
- 1 pinch freshly ground black pepper
- 1/2 teaspoon dried oregano

DIRECTIONS

1. Combine the olive oil, vinegar, garlic, oregano, mustard, salt and pepper in a jar with a tight fitting lid. Shake well before serving. Store in the refrigerator.

HABANERO PEPPER JELLY

Servings: 64 | Prep: 30m | Cooks: 20m | Total: 4h50m

NUTRITION FACTS

Calories: 82 | Carbohydrates: 20.8g | Fat: 0g | Protein: 0.1g | Cholesterol: 0mg

INGREDIENTS

- 8 half pint canning jars with lids and rings
- 1/2 cup minced red bell pepper
- 1 1/2 cups cider vinegar
- 15 habanero peppers, seeded and minced
- 6 1/2 cups white sugar
- 2 (3 ounce) pouches liquid pectin
- 1 cup shredded carrot

DIRECTIONS

1. Stir the vinegar and sugar in a saucepan over medium-high heat until the sugar has dissolved, then stir in the carrot and red bell pepper. Bring to a boil, reduce heat to medium, and simmer 5 minutes. Add the habanero peppers and simmer 5 minutes longer. Pour in the pectin, and boil for 1 minute, stirring constantly. Skim and discard any foam from the jelly.
2. Sterilize the jars and lids in boiling water for at least 5 minutes. Pour the jelly into the hot, sterilized jars, filling the jars to within 1/4 inch of the top. Wipe the rims of the jars with a moist paper towel to remove any food residue. Top with lids, and screw on rings.
3. Place a rack in the bottom of a large stockpot and fill halfway with water. Bring to a boil over high heat, then carefully lower the jars into the pot using a holder. Leave a 2 inch space between the jars. Pour in more boiling water if necessary until the water level is at least 1 inch above the tops of the jars. Bring the water to a full boil, cover the pot, and process for 5 minutes.
4. Remove the jars from the stockpot and place onto a cloth-covered or wood surface, several inches apart, until cool. Once cool, press the top of each lid with a finger, ensuring that the seal is tight (lid does not move up or down at all).

SMOKED PAPRIKA VINAIGRETTE

Servings: 12 | Prep: 10m | Cooks: 1h | Total: 1h10m

NUTRITION FACTS

Calories: 116 | Carbohydrates: 9.4g | Fat: 9.1g | Protein: 0.2g | Cholesterol: 0mg

INGREDIENTS

- 1/2 cup red wine vinegar
- 1 1/4 teaspoons smoked paprika
- 1/3 cup honey

- 1 clove garlic
- 1 tablespoon stone-ground mustard
- 2 tablespoons chopped onion
- 1 tablespoon lime juice
- 1/4 teaspoon oregano
- 3/4 teaspoon ground black pepper
- 1 pinch white sugar (optional)
- 3/4 teaspoon salt
- 1/2 cup olive oil

DIRECTIONS

1. Blend the red wine vinegar, honey, mustard, lime juice, pepper, salt, paprika, garlic, onion, oregano, and sugar together in a blender until thoroughly mixed. Drizzle the olive oil into the mixture while blending on low. Chill at least 1 hour before serving.

HONEY DIJON BALSAMIC VINAIGRETTE

Servings: 8 | Prep: 5m | Cooks: 0m | Total: 5m

NUTRITION FACTS

Calories: 138 | Carbohydrates: 4.5g | Fat: 13.5g | Protein: 0g | Cholesterol: 0mg

INGREDIENTS

- 1/3 cup balsamic vinegar
- 1 tablespoon honey
- 1/2 cup olive oil
- salt and pepper to taste
- 2 tablespoons Dijon mustard

DIRECTIONS

1. Whisk balsamic vinegar, olive oil, mustard, honey, salt, and pepper in a bowl.

CREAMY HOLLANDAISE SAUCE

Servings: 4 | Prep: 5m | Cooks: 10m | Total: 15m

NUTRITION FACTS

Calories: 464 | Carbohydrates: 2g | Fat: 50.4g | Protein: 3.2g | Cholesterol: 327mg

INGREDIENTS

- 4 egg yolks
- 1 tablespoon water
- 3 1/2 tablespoons lemon juice
- 1 cup butter, melted
- 1 pinch ground white pepper
- 1/4 teaspoon salt
- 1/8 teaspoon Worcestershire sauce

DIRECTIONS

1. Fill the bottom of a double boiler part-way with water. Make sure that water does not touch the top pan. Bring water to a gentle simmer. In the top of the double boiler, whisk together egg yolks, lemon juice, white pepper, Worcestershire sauce, and 1 tablespoon water.
2. Add the melted butter to egg yolk mixture 1 or 2 tablespoons at a time while whisking yolks constantly. If hollandaise begins to get too thick, add a teaspoon or two of hot water. Continue whisking until all butter is incorporated. Whisk in salt, then remove from heat. Place a lid on pan to keep sauce warm until ready to serve.

POPPYSEED DRESSING
Servings: 14 | Prep: 15m | Cooks: 0m | Total: 15m

NUTRITION FACTS

Calories: 161 | Carbohydrates: 5g | Fat: 15.9g | Protein: 0.2g | Cholesterol: 0mg

INGREDIENTS

- 1/3 cup white sugar
- 1 teaspoon grated onion
- 1/2 cup white vinegar
- 1 cup vegetable oil
- 1 teaspoon salt
- 1 tablespoon poppy seeds
- 1 teaspoon ground dry mustard

DIRECTIONS

1. In a blender or food processor, combine sugar, vinegar, salt, mustard and onion and process for 20 seconds. With blender or food processor on high, gradually add oil in a slow, steady stream. Stir in poppy seeds.

SECRET BURGER SAUCE
Servings: 12 | Prep: 10m | Cooks: 0m | Total: 10m

NUTRITION FACTS

Calories: 73 | Carbohydrates: 2g | Fat: 7.3g | Protein: 0.3g | Cholesterol: 3mg

INGREDIENTS

- 1/2 cup mayonnaise
- 1 teaspoon garlic powder
- 1/4 cup ketchup
- 1/2 teaspoon black pepper
- 1/2 cup chopped dill pickles

DIRECTIONS

1. Stir together the mayonnaise, ketchup, pickles, garlic powder, and pepper in a bowl, and place a dollop on your hamburger.

BASIL VINAIGRETTE DRESSING
Servings: 12 | Prep: 10m | Cooks: 0m | Total: 10m

NUTRITION FACTS

Calories: 183 | Carbohydrates: 6.1g | Fat: 18g | Protein: 0.1g | Cholesterol: 0mg

INGREDIENTS

- 1 cup olive oil
- 3 tablespoons chopped fresh basil
- 1/3 cup apple cider vinegar
- 2 cloves garlic, minced
- 1/4 cup honey

DIRECTIONS

1. In a bowl, whisk together the olive oil, apple cider vinegar, honey, basil, and garlic. Pour over or toss with your favorite salad to serve.

ABSOLUTELY AWESOME BBQ SAUCE
Servings: 16 | Prep: 10m | Cooks: 30m | Total: 55m

NUTRITION FACTS

Calories: 81 | Carbohydrates: 16.1g | Fat: 0.1g | Protein: 0.5g | Cholesterol: 0mg

INGREDIENTS

- 1 cup brown sugar
- 1/4 cup Worcestershire sauce
- 1/2 cup chile sauce
- 2 cloves garlic, crushed
- 1/2 cup rum
- 1 teaspoon ground dry mustard
- 1/4 cup soy sauce
- ground black pepper to taste
- 1/4 cup ketchup

DIRECTIONS

1. In a saucepan over low heat, mix the brown sugar, chile sauce, rum, soy sauce, ketchup, Worcestershire sauce, garlic, dry mustard, and pepper. Simmer 30 minutes, stirring occasionally. Cool, and refrigerate until ready to use.

SCOTT'S BUFFALO WING SAUCE
Servings: 5 | Prep: 5m | Cooks: 20m | Total: 25m

NUTRITION FACTS

Calories: 205 | Carbohydrates: 11.2g | Fat: 18.5g | Protein: 0.6g | Cholesterol: 49mg

INGREDIENTS

- 1/2 cup butter
- 1/3 cup hot pepper sauce
- 1/3 cup ketchup
- 2 tablespoons honey

DIRECTIONS

1. Combine the butter, hot sauce, ketchup, and honey in a small saucepan. Bring to a boil over medium-high heat. Reduce heat to low and simmer for 15 minutes. Use as a sauce for cooked chicken wings or pieces.

POP'S DILL PICKLES
Servings: 35 | Prep: 30m | Cooks: 15m | Total: 2h45m

NUTRITION FACTS

Calories: 35 | Carbohydrates: 8.5g | Fat: 0.1g | Protein: 0.7g | Cholesterol: 0mg

INGREDIENTS

- 8 pounds small pickling cucumbers
- 3 tablespoons pickling spice, wrapped in cheesecloth
- 4 cups water
- 7 1-quart canning jars with lids and rings
- 4 cups distilled white vinegar
- 7 heads fresh dill
- 3/4 cup white sugar
- 7 cloves garlic
- 1/2 cup pickling salt

DIRECTIONS

1. Place cucumbers in a large pot and cover with ice cubes. Let them sit for at least 2 hours but no more than 8. Drain and pat dry.
2. Place the water, vinegar, sugar, pickling salt, and pickling spice into a saucepan. Bring to boil, then simmer for 15 minutes.
3. Sterilize the jars and lids in boiling water for at least 5 minutes. Pack the cucumbers into the hot, sterilized jars, filling the jars to within 1/2 inch of the top. Place 1 dill head and 1 clove of garlic into each jar. Pour the hot pickling liquid into the jars, filling to within 1/4 inch of the rim. Wipe the rims of the jars with a moist paper towel to remove any food residue. Top with lids, and screw on rings.
4. Place a rack in the bottom of a large stockpot and fill halfway with water. Bring to a boil over high heat, then carefully lower the jars into the pot using a holder. Leave a 2 inch space between the jars. Pour in more boiling water if necessary until the water level is at least 1 inch above the tops of the jars. Bring the water to a full boil, cover the pot, and process for 5 minutes, or the time recommended by your county Extension agent.
5. Remove the jars from the stockpot and place onto a cloth-covered or wood surface, several inches apart, until cool. Once cool, press the top of each lid with a finger, ensuring that the seal is tight (lid does not move up or down at all). If any jars have not sealed properly, refrigerate them and eat within two weeks. Store in a cool, dark area, and wait at least 1 week before opening.

FISH TACO SAUCE
Servings: 6 | Prep: 10m | Cooks: 0m | Total: 10m

NUTRITION FACTS

Calories: 50 | Carbohydrates: 0.9g | Fat: 5.2g | Protein: 0.3g | Cholesterol: 5mg

INGREDIENTS

- 3 tablespoons sour cream
- 1/2 teaspoon garlic powder
- 2 tablespoons mayonnaise
- 1/2 teaspoon sriracha hot sauce
- 1 tablespoon lime juice

DIRECTIONS

1. Mix sour cream, mayonnaise, lime juice, garlic powder, and sriracha hot sauce together in a bowl until smooth.

CLASSIC HOLLANDAISE SAUCE
Servings: 6 | Prep: 2m | Cooks: 8m | Total: 10m

NUTRITION FACTS

Calories: 165 | Carbohydrates: 1.5g | Fat: 17.6g | Protein: 1.6g | Cholesterol: 143mg

INGREDIENTS

- 3 egg yolks
- 1 teaspoon salt
- 1/2 lemon, juiced
- 1 teaspoon ground black pepper
- 1 teaspoon cold water
- 1/2 cup butter

DIRECTIONS

1. In a small bowl, whisk together egg yolks, lemon juice, cold water, salt and pepper. Melt butter in a saucepan over low heat. Gradually whisk yolk mixture into butter. Continue whisking over low heat for 8 minutes, or until sauce is thickened. Serve immediately.

PEAR HONEY
Servings: 64 | Prep: 45m | Cooks: 3h | Total: 3h45m

NUTRITION FACTS

Calories: 111 | Carbohydrates: 28.7g | Fat: 0g | Protein: 0.1g | Cholesterol: 0mg

INGREDIENTS

- 8 cups peeled, cored and chopped pears
- 1 cup unsweetened pineapple juice
- 8 cups white sugar

DIRECTIONS

1. Place chopped pears into a large pot, and pour pineapple juice over them to prevent them from browning. Stir in sugar, and bring to a boil over medium-high heat. Stir frequently to prevent

scorching. When the pears are at a full boil, reduce heat to medium, and cook until the mixture is the color and texture of honey. The longer you cook it, the thicker it gets. Cooking time is usually 2 to 3 hours.

2. Ladle into hot sterile jars, filling to within 1/4 inch of the top. Wipe rims with a clean damp cloth, and seal jars with lids and rings. Process in a boiling water canner for 10 minutes, or the amount of time recommended by your local extension for your area.

BEST PORK CHOP MARINADE
Servings: 2 | Prep: 10m | Cooks: 6h | Total: 6h10m | Additional: 6h

NUTRITION FACTS

Calories: 756 | Carbohydrates: 29.6g | Fat: 41.7g | Protein: 62.1g | Cholesterol: 160mg

INGREDIENTS

- 2 large pork chops
- 1 teaspoon onion powder
- 1/4 cup extra-virgin olive oil
- 1 teaspoon Worcestershire sauce
- 3 tablespoons dark brown sugar
- 1 teaspoon white wine vinegar
- 2 tablespoons lemon juice
- 1 teaspoon mesquite-flavored seasoning
- 2 tablespoons spicy brown mustard
- 1/2 teaspoon dried parsley flakes
- 4 cloves garlic, chopped
- 1/2 teaspoon kosher salt
- 2 teaspoons dried thyme
- 1/2 teaspoon freshly ground black pepper

DIRECTIONS

1. Cut each pork chop from one side through the middle horizontally to within 1/2 inch of the other side. Open the two sides and spread them out like an open book.

2. Whisk olive oil, brown sugar, lemon juice, mustard, garlic, thyme, onion powder, Worcestershire sauce, vinegar, mesquite seasoning, parsley, salt, and pepper together in a bowl and pour into a large resealable plastic bag. Add pork chops, coat with the marinade, squeeze out excess air, and seal the bag. Marinate in the refrigerator, 6 to 8 hours.

BLACKENED SEASONING MIX
Servings: 12 | Prep: 5m | Cooks: 0m | Total: 5m

NUTRITION FACTS

Calories: 9 | Carbohydrates: 2g | Fat: 0.2g | Protein: 0.4g | Cholesterol: 0mg

INGREDIENTS

- 1 1/2 tablespoons paprika
- 1 teaspoon ground black pepper
- 1 tablespoon garlic powder
- 1 teaspoon cayenne pepper
- 1 tablespoon onion powder
- 1 teaspoon dried basil
- 1 tablespoon ground dried thyme
- 1 teaspoon dried oregano

DIRECTIONS

1. Combine the paprika, garlic powder, onion powder, thyme, black pepper, cayenne pepper, basil, and oregano in a bowl unti.

KATHY'S AWARD WINNING BARBEQUE SAUCE
Servings: 16 | Prep: 20m | Cooks: 1h | Total: 1h20m

NUTRITION FACTS

Calories: 102 | Carbohydrates: 22.3g | Fat: 1.8g | Protein: 0.5g | Cholesterol: 0mg

INGREDIENTS

- 1 cup ketchup
- 1 teaspoon ground black pepper
- 1 tablespoon Worcestershire sauce
- 1 teaspoon cayenne pepper
- 1 cup molasses
- 2 tablespoons lemon juice
- 2 tablespoons brown sugar
- 1 (5.5 ounce) can tomato juice
- 1/4 cup chopped onion
- 2 tablespoons liquid smoke flavoring
- 1 tablespoon garlic powder

DIRECTIONS

1. In a blender or food processor, combine the ketchup, Worcestershire sauce, molasses, brown sugar, onion, garlic powder, ground black pepper, cayenne pepper, lemon juice, tomato juice, and liquid smoke flavoring. Puree until smooth, and transfer to a saucepan.
2. Place saucepan on the stove over medium heat. Bring mixture to a boil, reduce heat to low, and simmer for about 1 hour, or to desired thickness.

JAPANESE GINGER SALAD DRESSING
Servings: 12 | Prep: 5m | Cooks: 0m | Total: 5m

NUTRITION FACTS

Calories: 170 | Carbohydrates: 3g | Fat: 18g | Protein: 0.5g | Cholesterol: 0mg

INGREDIENTS

- 1 cup olive oil
- 3 tablespoons minced fresh ginger root
- 1/4 cup soy sauce
- 1 teaspoon prepared Dijon-style mustard
- 1 lemon, juiced
- 2 teaspoons honey
- 3 cloves garlic, minced
- ground black pepper to taste

DIRECTIONS

1. In a small bowl, whisk together the soy sauce, lemon juice, garlic, ginger, mustard, honey and pepper. Once these are thoroughly combined, add the oil in a steady stream, whisking constantly. When all of the oil is incorporated into the dressing, pour into a glass jar and chill until serving.

BEST CAROLINA BBQ MEAT SAUCE
Servings: 12 | Prep: 10m | Cooks: 40m | Total: 8h55m | Additional: 8h5m

NUTRITION FACTS

Calories: 92 | Carbohydrates: 12.2g | Fat: 3.9g | Protein: 1.6g | Cholesterol: 5mg

INGREDIENTS

- 1 1/2 cups prepared yellow mustard
- 1 teaspoon freshly ground white pepper
- 1/2 cup packed brown sugar
- 1/2 teaspoon cayenne pepper
- 3/4 cup cider vinegar

- 1 1/2 teaspoons Worcestershire sauce
- 3/4 cup beer
- 2 tablespoons butter, room temperature
- 1 tablespoon chili powder
- 1 1/2 teaspoons liquid smoke flavoring
- 1 teaspoon freshly ground black pepper
- 1 teaspoon Louisiana-style hot sauce, or to taste

DIRECTIONS

1. In a heavy non-reactive saucepan, stir together the mustard, brown sugar, vinegar, and beer. Season with chili powder and black, white, and cayenne peppers. Bring to a simmer over medium-low heat, and cook for about 20 minutes. DO NOT BOIL, or you will scorch the sugar and peppers.
2. Mix in the Worcestershire sauce, butter, and liquid smoke. Simmer for another 15 to 20 minutes. Taste, and season with hot sauce to your liking. Pour into an airtight jar, and refrigerate for overnight to allow flavors to blend. The vinegar taste may be a little strong until the sauce completely cools.

TZATZIKI SAUCE (YOGURT AND CUCUMBER DIP)
Servings: 16 | Prep: 25m | Cooks: 10h | Total: 10h25m

NUTRITION FACTS

Calories: 21 | Carbohydrates: 2.8g | Fat: 0.5g | Protein: 1.6g | Cholesterol: 2mg

INGREDIENTS

- 1 (16 ounce) container low-fat plain yogurt
- 1 tablespoon chopped fresh mint
- 1 cucumber, peeled, seeded, and grated
- 1 tablespoon fresh lemon juice
- 1 clove garlic, minced
- salt and pepper to taste
- 1 tablespoon chopped fresh parsley

DIRECTIONS

1. Line a colander with two layers of cheesecloth and place it over a medium bowl. Place the yogurt on the cheesecloth and cover the colander with plastic wrap. Allow yogurt to drain overnight.
2. Lay grated cucumber on a plate lined with paper towel; allow to drain 1 to 2 hours.
3. Combine the drained yogurt, cucumber, garlic, parsley, mint, lemon juice, salt, and pepper in a bowl. Refrigerate for at least 2 hours before serving.

AMAZING SUN-DRIED TOMATO CREAM SAUCE

Servings: 4 | Prep: 5m | Cooks: 10m | Total: 15m

NUTRITION FACTS

Calories: 349 | Carbohydrates: 4.3g | Fat: 34.8g | Protein: 6.7g | Cholesterol: 116mg

INGREDIENTS

- 1 cup heavy cream
- 1/4 cup chopped sun-dried tomatoes
- 3 tablespoons butter
- salt and pepper to taste
- 1/2 cup shredded mozzarella cheese
- 1 tablespoon pine nuts
- 2 tablespoons grated Parmesan cheese

DIRECTIONS

1. Heat the cream and butter in a saucepan over medium heat until almost boiling, but do not boil. Add mozzarella and Parmesan cheeses, and stir until melted. Stir in the sun-dried tomatoes, and season with salt and pepper. Remove from heat and serve over pasta with a sprinkling of pine nuts.

FRANK'S FAMOUS SPAGHETTI SAUCE

Servings: 8 | Prep: 15m | Cooks: 30m | Total: 45m

NUTRITION FACTS

Calories: 168 | Carbohydrates: 15.6g | Fat: 6.8g | Protein: 13.3g | Cholesterol: 45mg

INGREDIENTS

- 1 tablespoon olive oil
- 1 pinch dried basil
- 1 onion, chopped
- 1 pinch dried oregano
- 1 green bell pepper, chopped
- ground black pepper to taste
- 3 cloves garlic, minced
- 1 (14.5 ounce) can stewed tomatoes
- 4 fresh mushrooms, sliced
- 2 (15 ounce) cans tomato sauce
- 1 pound ground turkey
- 1 (6 ounce) can tomato paste

DIRECTIONS

1. In a large skillet over medium heat, saute onions, green bell pepper and garlic in olive oil until onions are translucent and the peppers are tender. Add the mushrooms, ground turkey, basil, oregano and ground black pepper; fry stirring frequently until the turkey is done.
2. Add the can of stewed tomatoes with liquid and reduce heat; simmering until the tomatoes are soft and begin to fall apart. Add the tomato sauce and stir; add tomato paste to thicken. Simmer on very low heat for about 15 minutes. Serve over you favorite pasta.

RUM SAUCE
Servings: 10 | Prep: 5m | Cooks: 5m | Total: 10m

NUTRITION FACTS

Calories: 84 | Carbohydrates: 11.9g | Fat: 2.8g | Protein: 0.8g | Cholesterol: 8mg

INGREDIENTS

- 2 tablespoons butter
- 1 cup milk
- 1 tablespoon cornstarch
- 3 tablespoons white or dark rum
- 1/2 cup sugar

DIRECTIONS

1. Melt butter in a small saucepan over medium heat. Mix together the sugar and cornstarch, and stir into the butter. Pour in milk, and cook stirring frequently until the mixture begins to boil. Continue cooking until thick, stirring constantly. Remove from heat, and stir in rum. Serve warm.

'OUT OF SALAD DRESSING' SALAD DRESSING
Servings: 12 | Prep: 10m | Cooks: 0m | Total: 8h10m | Additional: 8h

NUTRITION FACTS

Calories: 146 | Carbohydrates: 2g | Fat: 13.7g | Protein: 4g | Cholesterol: 14mg

INGREDIENTS

- 1 1/2 lemons, juiced
- 3/4 cup mayonnaise
- 1 cup freshly grated Parmesan cheese
- 1 cup milk
- 2 teaspoons garlic salt

DIRECTIONS

1. Mix together lemon juice, parmesan cheese, garlic salt, and mayonnaise until smooth. Stir in milk, adjusting the amount or adding a little water, to make the dressing as thin or thick as you like. Cover and refrigerate 8 hours, or overnight.

HONEY GARLIC VINAIGRETTE

Servings: 8 | Prep: 10m | Cooks: 0m | Total: 10m

NUTRITION FACTS

Calories: 268 | Carbohydrates: 6.8g | Fat: 27.3g | Protein: 0.1g | Cholesterol: 0mg

INGREDIENTS

- 1 cup vegetable oil
- 1/3 cup apple cider vinegar
- 3 tablespoons honey
- 2 cloves garlic, minced

DIRECTIONS

1. In a container, combine oil, vinegar, honey, and garlic. Cover, and shake until blended. Set aside for 45 minutes, to allow flavors to combine. Shake again before serving.

HOT PEANUT SAUCE

Servings: 6 | Prep: 10m | Cooks: 0m | Total: 10m

NUTRITION FACTS

Calories: 80 | Carbohydrates: 6g | Fat: 5.5g | Protein: 3.1g | Cholesterol: 0mg

INGREDIENTS

- 4 tablespoons peanut butter
- 1 1/2 tablespoons brown sugar
- 4 tablespoons hot water
- 1/4 teaspoon cayenne pepper
- 2 tablespoons soy sauce
- 1 1/2 teaspoons lemon juice

DIRECTIONS

1. In a small bowl combine peanut butter and water; mix until a smooth paste forms. Stir in soy sauce, then brown sugar, cayenne and lemon juice. Mix by hand until well combined and smooth.

SIMPLE MAPLE SYRUP
Servings: 6 | Prep: 5m | Cooks: 5m | Total: 10m

NUTRITION FACTS

Calories: 259 | Carbohydrates: 66.7g | Fat: 0g | Protein: 0g | Cholesterol: 0mg

INGREDIENTS

- 2 cups white sugar
- 1 cup boiling water
- 1/2 teaspoon maple flavored extract

DIRECTIONS

1. In a saucepan, combine sugar and water. Cook and stir until sugar is dissolved. Remove from heat, and stir in maple flavoring. Serve warm.

TARTAR SAUCE
Servings: 40 | Prep: 15m | Cooks: 0m | Total: 15m

NUTRITION FACTS

Calories: 161 | Carbohydrates: 1.4g | Fat: 17.5g | Protein: 0.3g | Cholesterol: 8mg

INGREDIENTS

- 1 quart mayonnaise
- 1/4 cup lemon juice
- 1 cup diced onion
- 1 cup finely chopped dill pickle

DIRECTIONS

1. In a stainless steel or glass mixing bowl, combine the mayonnaise, lemon juice, onion, and dill pickle. Mix thoroughly. Transfer to a glass or plastic container with a tight lid and refrigerate.

HOLLANDAISE SAUCE
Servings: 4 | Prep: 5m | Cooks: 15m | Total: 20m

NUTRITION FACTS

Calories: 450 | Carbohydrates: 1.4g | Fat: 49.4g | Protein: 2.5g | Cholesterol: 276mg

INGREDIENTS

- 3 egg yolks
- 3/4 cup unsalted butter, melted
- 1 1/2 tablespoons fresh lemon juice
- salt to taste
- 4 tablespoons unsalted butter, chilled
- 1 teaspoon ground white pepper

DIRECTIONS

1. Add egg yolks to a small saucepan; whisk until lemon yellow and slightly thick, about 1 minute. Whisk in lemon juice.
2. Add 2 tablespoons cold butter, and place over very low heat. Whisk constantly while butter is melting, and continue whisking until thick enough to see the pan between strokes. Remove pan from heat, and beat in 1 tablespoon cold butter. Repeat. Whisk in melted butter a little bit at a time. Season with salt and white pepper to taste.

DESSERTLOVER'S CLASSIC CARAMEL SAUCE

Servings: 16 | Prep: 10m | Cooks: 15m | Total: 55m | Additional : 30m

NUTRITION FACTS

Calories: 150 | Carbohydrates: 19.3g | Fat: 8.3g | Protein: 0.4g | Cholesterol: 29mg

INGREDIENTS

- 1/3 cup water
- 1 1/4 cups heavy cream
- 1 1/2 cups white sugar
- 1/2 teaspoon vanilla extract
- 2 tablespoons unsalted butter
- 1 pinch salt

DIRECTIONS

1. Bring the water, sugar, and butter to a simmer in a saucepan over medium heat. Do not stir the mixture until the sugar has completely dissolved in the water. Cook uncovered, stirring occasionally, until the caramel has turned golden brown, 5 to 10 minutes.
2. Carefully pour in a slow, steady stream of cream into the caramel while stirring constantly. The hot caramel will boil vigorously when the cream is added and solidify in areas. Add the vanilla extract and salt. Continue stirring over low heat until the caramel is smooth and creamy, 5 to 10 minutes more. Allow to cool for at least half an hour before using.

BRANDIED ORANGE AND CRANBERRY SAUCE

Servings: 8 | Prep: 5m | Cooks: 20m | Total: 25m

NUTRITION FACTS

Calories: 236 | Carbohydrates: 59.5g | Fat: 0.1g | Protein: 0.4g | Cholesterol: 0mg

INGREDIENTS

- 2/3 cup orange zest
- 1 tablespoon lemon juice
- 2 cups water
- 3 cups cranberries
- 2 cups white sugar
- 1 tablespoon brandy
- 2/3 cup orange juice

DIRECTIONS

1. In a small pan over medium heat, combine the orange zest and water. Cover and bring to boil. Reduce heat and simmer for 15 minutes. Drain, reserving zest and 1/3 cup liquid.
2. To the reserved liquid, add the sugar, orange juice and lemon juice. Bring to boil; reduce heat and simmer for 3 minutes uncovered, stirring often.
3. Add cranberries; increase heat to medium-high and boil for about 10 minutes or until the cranberries have popped and a small spoonful of sauce sets on a cold plate.
4. Remove from heat, stir in brandy. Pour into 4 1/2 pint jars leaving 1/2 inch space from top. Place lids onto jars, and store in the refrigerator for up to two weeks.

CRISP PICKLED GREEN BEANS

Servings: 48 | Prep: 1h | Cooks: 10m | Total: 1h10m

NUTRITION FACTS

Calories: 8 | Carbohydrates: 1.8g | Fat: 0g | Protein: 0.5g | Cholesterol: 0mg

INGREDIENTS

- 2 1/2 pounds fresh green beans
- 1 clove garlic, peeled
- 2 1/2 cups distilled white vinegar
- 1 bunch fresh dill weed
- 2 cups water
- 3/4 teaspoon red pepper flakes (optional)
- 1/4 cup salt

DIRECTIONS

1. Sterilize 6 (1/2 pint) jars with rings and lids and keep hot. Trim green beans to 1/4 inch shorter than your jars.
2. In a large saucepan, stir together the vinegar, water and salt. Add garlic and bring to a rolling boil over high heat. In each jar, place 1 sprig of dill and 1/8 teaspoon of red pepper flakes. Pack green beans into the jars so they are standing on their ends.
3. Ladle the boiling brine into the jars, filling to within 1/4 inch of the tops. Discard garlic. Seal jars with lids and rings. Place in a hot water bath so they are covered by 1 inch of water. Simmer but do not boil for 10 minutes to process. Cool to room temperature. Test jars for a good seal by pressing on the center of the lid. It should not move. Refrigerate any jars that do not seal properly. Let pickles ferment for 2 to 3 weeks before eating.

TERIYAKI SAUCE
Servings: 6 | Prep: 1m | Cooks: 0m | Total: 1m

NUTRITION FACTS

Calories: 42 | Carbohydrates: 8.3g | Fat: g | Protein: 1.8g | Cholesterol: 0mg

INGREDIENTS

- 2/3 cup soy sauce
- 1 teaspoon ground ginger
- 1/4 cup cooking sherry
- 1 clove garlic, minced
- 2 tablespoons white sugar

DIRECTIONS

1. In a small bowl, combine soy sauce, sherry, sugar, ginger, and garlic.

APPLESAUCE BARBEQUE SAUCE
Servings: 28 | Prep: 10m | Cooks: 20m | Total: 30m

NUTRITION FACTS

Calories: 49 | Carbohydrates: 12.6g | Fat: 0g | Protein: 0.1g | Cholesterol: 0mg

INGREDIENTS

- 1 cup applesauce
- 1/2 teaspoon ground black pepper
- 1/2 cup ketchup
- 1/2 teaspoon paprika

- 2 cups unpacked brown sugar
- 1/2 teaspoon garlic powder
- 6 tablespoons lemon juice
- 1/2 teaspoon ground cinnamon
- 1/2 teaspoon salt

DIRECTIONS

1. In a saucepan over medium heat, mix applesauce, ketchup, brown sugar, lemon juice, salt, pepper, paprika, garlic powder, and cinnamon. Bring mixture to a boil. Remove from heat, and cool completely. Use to baste the meat of your choice.

BATMAN'S BEST CAESAR DRESSING
Servings: 20 | Prep: 15m | Cooks: 0m | Total: 15m

NUTRITION FACTS

Calories: 165 | Carbohydrates: 1.3g | Fat: 17.4g | Protein: 1.4g | Cholesterol: 4mg

INGREDIENTS

- 1 1/2 cups olive oil
- 1/2 teaspoon mustard powder
- 1 tablespoon red wine vinegar
- 4 cloves garlic, crushed
- 1/4 cup lemon juice
- 3 tablespoons sour cream
- 1 tablespoon Worcestershire sauce
- 1/2 cup grated Parmesan cheese
- 2 tablespoons anchovy paste

DIRECTIONS

1. In a food processor or blender, combine the olive oil, vinegar, lemon juice, Worcestershire sauce, anchovy paste, mustard, garlic, sour cream and Parmesan cheese. Process until smooth. Pour into a glass container, seal, and refrigerate until ready to use.

STABILIZED WHIPPED CREAM ICING
Servings: 16 | Prep: 5m | Cooks: 3m | Total: 25m

NUTRITION FACTS

Calories: 1.2 | Carbohydrates: 1.2g | Fat: 5.5g | Protein: 0.4g | Cholesterol: 20mg

INGREDIENTS

- 1/4 cup cold water
- 1 tablespoon white sugar
- 1 teaspoon unflavored gelatin
- 1/2 teaspoon vanilla extract
- 1 cup heavy whipping cream

DIRECTIONS

1. Chill mixing bowl and beaters for at least 15 minutes before using. Place water in a small microwave-safe bowl. Sprinkle gelatin over water and allow to soften 5 minutes.
2. Dissolve gelatin by microwaving for 3 minutes, stirring after every minute. Remove from microwave and let stand at room temperature for 10 minutes; gelatin must be liquid but not warm when added to cream.
3. Remove bowl and beaters from refrigerator and pour in cream, sugar, and vanilla extract. Beat together just until beater marks begin to show distinctly.
4. Add gelatin mixture to cream, pouring in a steady stream while beating constantly. Beat until stiff peaks form. Use immediately.

Printed in Great Britain
by Amazon

41809345R00057